Mobile Marketing

How mobile technology is revolutionizing marketing, communications and advertising

Daniel Rowles

KoganPage

LONDON PHILADELPHIA NEW DELHI

First published in Great Britain and the United States in 2014 by Kogan Page Limited

2nd Floor, 45 Gee Street
London EC1V 3RS
United Kingdom
www.koganpage.com

1518 Walnut Street, Suite 1100
Philadelphia PA 19102
USA

4737/23 Ansari Road
Daryaganj
New Delhi 110002
India

© Daniel Rowles, 2014

The right of Daniel Rowles to be identified as the author of this work has been asserted by him in accordance with the Copyright, Designs and Patents Act 1988.

ISBN   978 0 7494 6938 2
E-ISBN   978 0 7494 6939 9

British Library Cataloguing-in-Publication Data

A CIP record for this book is available from the British Library.

Library of Congress Cataloging-in-Publication Data

Rowles, Daniel.
   Mobile marketing : how mobile technology is revolutionizing marketing, communications, and advertising / Daniel Rowles.
      pages cm
   ISBN 978-0-7494-6938-2 (pbk.) – ISBN 978-0-7494-6939-9 (ebook)   1. Internet marketing.
2. Internet advertising.   3. Mobile commerce.   4. Mobile communication systems.
5. Telemarketing.   I. Title.
   HF5415.1265.R69 2013
   658.8'72–dc23
                                                                                    2013032118

Typeset by Graphicraft Limited, Hong Kong
Print production managed by Jellyfish
Printed and bound in Great Britain by CPI Group (UK) Ltd, Croydon, CR0 4YY

This book is dedicated to my ever patient, beautiful and straight-talking wife Susana, without whom it would still be on a to-do list somewhere.

This is also a great opportunity to get my kids' names in print, so they can show all their friends and I can score many, many 'awesome dad' points. I love you both dearly, Teresa and Charlie.

CONTENTS

LIST OF FIGURES

FOREWORD

It's clear that mobile devices are having a profound impact not only on how we communicate on a daily basis, but also on how we interact and engage with individuals and organizations of all types.

At the Chartered Institute of Marketing (CIM) we see time and time again that practitioners, and those studying business of any type (whether they consider themselves marketers or not), need a better understanding of the digital landscape. We also see that landscape is changing incredibly quickly and that mobile is playing a major part of this.

In this fast-changing environment, knowledge of both the strategic impact and the tactical issues around mobile marketing will become increasingly important, particularly as this overlaps into areas such as social media.

Daniel has worked extensively with CIM, helping our members and customers to navigate their way through this exciting and fast-moving environment. He is a respected authority on all things digital and as such is the ideal guide for your mobile marketing journey.

Anne Godfrey, Chief Executive, CIM

ACKNOWLEDGEMENTS

There are many people who have encouraged and assisted me in writing this book and I have named a few of them here.

Firstly to the small and perfectly formed Target Internet team, Ciaran and Felice. Thanks to Ciaran for motivating and cajoling me to keep things on track generally, and for letting me steal his ideas (particularly on QR codes). Massive thanks to Felice for taking on all of my tricky (and often crappy) research tasks and completing them without any drama.

A huge thank you to the very inspirational and talented Jonathan Macdonald for making the introduction that led to this book. The free wine is on me next time we spend 12 hours in an airport lounge.

To all of the team at the CIM who have supported and assisted in my career for many years by being both professional colleagues and great friends. Special thanks to Anne Godfrey for her Foreword, and her trust, to Chris Moriarty for all of the bromance love, to Thomas Brown for the insights and laughs, and to Renita Shwili for sage advice and encouragement.

To the Econsultancy team for constantly challenging me, sending me to do interesting things and being professional and fun to work with. Special thanks to CEO Ashley Friedlein for his contribution and to Chris Clapham for always keeping me busy and on track.

And finally, a massive thank you to all of you who read this book, visit Target Internet, listen to the Digital Marketing podcast, follow me on Twitter and very kindly give me an audience with whom to engage and share my ideas.

Introduction

It has been 'the year of mobile marketing' for the last five years. Or so you would believe if you read many popular digital marketing blogs and journals. You may also believe that 'mobile marketing is dead' if you've been following any of the bloggers keen to create discussion. The truth lies somewhere in-between.

This book aims to be a practical guide to understanding and using mobile marketing for organizations of different types and sizes around the globe. However, in order to do this we need to start by defining what we really mean by mobile marketing.

Looking in the wrong direction

The most common mistake made in mobile marketing is to focus on the device. When we focus on the smartphone or tablet that someone is using we instantly start to look in the wrong direction. I'll explain why.

How big does a phone need to get before it becomes a tablet? What about if my laptop has a touch-screen? Does it then become a tablet? The reality is that the merging and extremely fast evolution of mobile devices is already out of date by the time we have adjusted to it.

What we need is a strategy and implementation plan that allows us to make maximum use of the technology available without getting bogged down with which devices we are planning for (although we will look at that later in this book).

Focus on the user journey

Mobile marketing is actually all about understanding the user journey. Understanding what individuals (even when acting as part of larger organizations) want to achieve. This could be anything from educating themselves to booking a cinema ticket, but whatever the objective, we need to understand how the technologies that make up mobile marketing can be used to help achieve the goals of an individual.

The human element

Our mobile devices are by nature very personal to us. We carry them with us, use them when we are moving from place to place and they help make our lives easier (or at least should do!) If I try and broadcast generic marketing messages through your mobile device they are even less likely to work than through other channels. Generally speaking, when you are on a mobile device you have less time, you are focussed on a specific goal and you are 'in the moment'. And this is exactly why mobile marketing is so essential and needs us to think about marketing in a very different way.

Disruption

As you work through this book you'll learn about the practicalities of building apps, mobile websites and technologies like near field communication (NFC). All we are really doing though is arming ourselves with tools for a world where the shift in marketing has been profound.

We'll explore how media consumption has radically changed, how people are using multiple screens at once (think how often you watch TV without a smartphone to hand) and how the idea of a mobile device starts to become obsolete when you are wearing those devices (we'll explore this later).

So what can we do in such a fast-changing and disruptive market? We focus on the basics.

Back to basics

I've worked with many of the world's largest and fastest changing organizations over the last 15 years, advising them how they can best use digital technologies to achieve their business objectives. No matter what the topic, be it social media search optimization or e-mail marketing (both of which are part of mobile marketing), I always come back to basics. Set your objectives, understand your target audience, select the appropriate tools, channels and content and then deploy, test and learn. It is the year of mobile marketing and mobile marketing is dead.

How to get the most out of this book

The book is split into three key sections:

1: Mobile marketing in perspective

This section will give you an understanding of who the mobile consumer is, a core view of the technology involved and how it impacts you, and finally how to set objectives for your mobile marketing.

2: Tactical toolkit

This section explores the core technologies, techniques and tools involved in mobile marketing. Here we explore things like QR codes, mobile sites, apps and NFC. Jump straight to this section if you need some hands-on tips and techniques.

3: Checklists

This short and final section will help you set a mobile strategy and make sure you aren't missing anything. It comprises some practical checklists and a step-by-step planning tool for creating your mobile strategy.

You can also get all the latest on mobile marketing by visiting **http://www.targetinternet.com/mobilemarketing**

PART ONE
Mobile marketing in perspective

Introduction

It's very easy to start thinking about mobile marketing from the perspective of the tactics we are planning to implement: that great idea for an app, a beautifully designed responsive website or a clever idea for using mobile payments. The reality, just with any digital marketing activity, is that it's generally a very good idea to take a step back and fully understand what we are trying to achieve and the environment we are working in.

Part One therefore is all about understanding the broader environment we are working in. It will help you understand who the mobile consumer is, get a core view of the technology involved and finally show you how to set objectives for your mobile marketing.

This core knowledge will help you inform your strategy before you start to embark on the tactical journey of implementing your mobile marketing campaigns (which is covered in detail in Part Two).

Although this section explores some of the latest statistics and developments in mobile marketing, we also acknowledge that this is a fast-paced environment with constant change. For that reason we have pointed out numerous resources along the way, as well as compiling the best of these on our website.

This first part of the book is also here to stop you wasting time and money by highlighting some of the key risks of mobile marketing. It is very easy to be seduced by new technologies that offer fantastic creative opportunities. However, without the grounding of how this fits into an overall strategy and a clear measurement framework to tie things back to our objectives, there is huge potential to be very busy without being productive in any way.

I still see, on an almost daily basis, Facebook pages for the sake of Facebook pages and mobile apps for the sake of apps. This generally starts in one of two ways. Either somebody senior says, 'Why don't we have an app? Go make an app!' or somebody comes up with a half-baked idea that starts its life without any proper planning. The end results are generally disappointing and costly. This then gives the impression that mobile is costly, complicated and ineffective. In reality, any marketing done in this way is generally a disaster.

This section, however, is not about looking at the negative. It's all about embracing the huge and exciting potential that mobile marketing offers and doing so in a risk-mitigated way. This will help you make the most of your resources and should save you a lot of stress.

What Part One will help you do

- Make sure you have a clear view of the environment you are working in.

- Understand how mobile makes up part of the user journey.

- Set your objectives and understand the mobile technologies that might help you achieve these objectives.

- Highlight some of the key risks you will face along your mobile marketing journey.

- Understand how to cope with a fast-changing environment and see how our website can help you stay up to date and on top of the latest developments: **http://www.targetinternet.com/mobilemarketing**.

Understanding the mobile consumer

We can now interact with businesses from pretty much anywhere we have some form of internet connection. On the bus, travelling by train or while walking along. This image of mobile marketing being all about mobility in its purest sense is often used, but defies the reality of how we are actually using mobile devices in the majority of cases. Most mobile usage is done at home, in the office or somewhere else stationary, and most of it is about 'me' time (*Harvard Business Review*, February 2013).

So if it's actually not about using your phone when moving, why is Hotels.com's 'Hotel Booked in Freefall' video so successful (attracting over 1 million views in YouTube at time of publishing) and often quoted as a great example, as it is in Google's excellent Mobile Playbook.

Well, first of all it's a fun and engaging concept that grabs your attention. Somebody trying to book a hotel room on a phone while jumping out of a plane is a fairly extreme idea! However, it achieves its objectives as a piece of marketing because it demonstrates and reinforces a key value proposition. That is the idea that Hotels.com makes it quick and easy to book hotels.

This alignment with value proposition and what the consumer actually wants is essential, and although it sounds obvious, is more often than not completely missed in mobile marketing campaigns. The reason that this basic concept of alignment with consumer requirements is missed is that we (or the partners and agencies we work with) are blinded by the technology and creative options.

The consumer and business-to-business

Very often when we talk about 'mobile consumers' we immediately start to think about somebody buying a product in a shop or a website. However, I think we should look at the consumer in a broader context, and part of this will include anyone that is engaging with our mobile marketing in some way.

For this reason when we talk about the mobile consumer, we will also be considering those making business-to-business (B2B) purchasing decisions. Clearly the requirements of somebody checking the reviews of a movie are very different to those of somebody checking information on the supplier they are about to meet, but they do hold the same principle in common. That is, that we need to understand what this consumer is trying to achieve and in what context.

In many cases mobile marketing is dismissed in the B2B environment as something that is more suited to business-to-consumer (B2C) marketing, but I would argue that the whole point of mobile is its personal nature and the need to understand the target audience's objectives and context.

Business users mix their personal and business time on mobile devices, and with social platforms like LinkedIn it is possible for this line to become even further blurred. I may be relaxing and staying up to date with my social contacts and I may be looking at the LinkedIn app as part of this, for example.

We clearly need to look at B2B and B2C marketing differently, but many of the same core principles apply. At the core of this is understanding our target users' needs and context, then using mobile marketing to service these needs and making sure they align with our business objectives.

Technology for the sake of technology

Just because we can build an app doesn't mean we should (in fact you really need to think about mobile sites before apps in the majority of cases, but more on that later). Using technology inappropriately without setting objectives or having a clear business case is nothing new.

From my experience, the majority of business Twitter and Facebook accounts are set up with little or no idea whatsoever of why they're being created. It happens because somebody senior has decided it's a good idea without understanding it, somebody junior did it without asking anyone, or someone in the business has seen competitors are doing it so feel an opportunity is being missed. It doesn't mean it's necessarily the wrong channel or a bad idea, but anything done without objectives or a business case is generally doomed to failure.

This lack of strategy isn't isolated to mobile marketing. One of my favourite examples demonstrates how this applies to digital marketing generally. Dave Chaffey is a well-respected digital marketing author (as well as being an excellent lecturer, public speaker and someone whose opinion I respect). He runs a website called SmartInsights.com that provides digital marketing advice and stimulates conversation on the topic. As such he regularly asks his audience how many of them are carrying out any form of digital marketing and how many of them have a strategy behind this activity. Every time this questionnaire is run, the results come back the same. Nearly 70 per cent of those asked are carrying out digital marketing activities with no strategy. Although this is only a small sample survey, it does identify a key trend that I can back up from my many years of working with organizations to improve their digital marketing efforts.

Now, to be fair, this 70 per cent might be doing the right things, for the right reason, measuring effectively and achieving their business objectives. Although I'm pretty sure that's not the case for all of them. Even if it was, they probably wouldn't know it, as they have no strategy to measure their success against.

User journey and context

Understanding the user journey is going to be essential to the success of our mobile marketing, so let's try and understand this in a bit more detail. We need to understand what our target audience might want to achieve, understand their path to doing this, see how mobile fits in, and then provide the right experiences and content to achieve these objectives.

Some of this will be the 'discovery phase' (also referred to as push, stimulus and in a dozen other ways!) where we are trying to build awareness, educate and stimulate some form of further action.

TABLE 2.1   Discovery and engagement phases in mobile marketing

Discovery Phase	Engagement Phase
Mobile e-mail	Mobile sites
Mobile display ads	Apps
Mobile paid search	Mobile-optimized social
Mobile organic search	Mobile payment and couponing
Offline stimulus (QR codes etc)	Location-based interaction (NFC etc)
Push notifications	

Some will be in the 'engagement phase'. These are activities that are driving engagement, experiences and moving toward the users' final objectives.

The different techniques and technologies are shown in Table 2.1, and we'll explore them in more detail in Part Two of this book. However, we first need to identify how they fit together.

The line between discovery and engagement becomes increasingly blurred as we move into location-based interaction (engaging with a brand when in-store for example), but these phases can start to lay a foundation for us when thinking about where mobile fits into the user journey. However, this is currently a fairly one-dimensional model that only really talks about mobile marketing techniques, while acknowledging that things like offline marketing may exist.

Mobile and multi-channel marketing

The reality of all marketing is that there generally isn't one thing that makes you buy a product or choose a supplier. Generally there are a huge range of factors that make you prefer one brand over another, choose a supplier or buy a particular detergent. Marketing is all about understanding this process.

As marketers we can model, measure and use all sorts of tools to try and understand this buying process, and this is where digital marketing has its greatest strengths. We have access to more data and more capability to measure the user journey than ever before. However, the missing piece in this measurement puzzle has been the interaction between online and offline marketing. We'll still face some challenges with this, but quite often mobile can act as the bridge between offline and online.

Mobile marketing will generally be part of the user journey and many other channels may be involved, some digital and some not. The journey is very unlikely to be a linear one, and many channels and types of content may be re-visited several times, in no particular order, and we may not have any visibility on many of the steps in the journey.

User journey examples

Let's take a look at two real-world user journeys all the way through to purchase and consider how different channels are working together.

Business-to-business example

I need a new hosting company for my business website. I'm responsible for the website's reliability and I have had some bad experiences previously, ending in my website being down and me being frustrated and embarrassed. This buying decision is primarily motivated by risk mitigation, but I also need to make sure that my website will be fast and any provider will give me the opportunity to expand and improve my web offering, so I need flexibility and performance. This is not a decision I will make without being well informed and the user journey is made up of multiple steps, including, but not limited to:

- doing numerous searches for suppliers;
- reading online reviews of these suppliers;
- signing up for newsletters from each of these suppliers;

- asking opinions from my social network on LinkedIn and Twitter of their experiences;

- completing several diagnostic tools to understand what kind of hosting I actually need;

- reading websites that talk about the technology behind hosting to educate myself about the technology;

- signing up for newsletters from the sites that helped me educate myself;

- talking to colleagues and trusted partners at unrelated events and meetings;

- getting recommendations for suppliers I had never heard of and making a note on my phone.

On first inspection, the only step in this journey that specifically used a mobile device was making a note of recommended suppliers. The reality however is that a great deal of this research was actually done when I was in a hotel, travelling by train or on a plane. I also use multiple devices, including a laptop, a tablet and a smartphone.

So let's map out what's important to note in this user journey. Firstly, that my decision is being based on risk mitigation and finding the right fit to my needs. I also need to educate myself on the topic (which is very common in B2B buying decisions).

We also need to note the practicalities of this journey. It was done almost entirely online, except where face-to-face word of mouth was involved. However, I only knew to search for several suppliers because I was already aware of them due to some other offline inter-action at previous trade shows. Also, much of the time I was reading and educating myself I was actually offline as I had no internet access (on a plane or on a train with poor connectivity).

So what does this tell us about our mobile marketing planning? Well, our value proposition needs to align closely with the ideas of risk mitigation, trust and education. So a clear value proposition aligned to user needs at the heart of any strategy would be essential for any potential supplier.

The suppliers needed to provide more content than just telling me how great their solution was. I needed education to build trust. This is a classic example of the need for content marketing, which we'll discuss shortly.

I had relied on my social network and online reviews heavily to influence my decision. An effective social media approach was also clearly going to be essential for any potential supplier, and how I experienced this on different devices would need to be considered.

As well as needing these different types of content I needed to be able to consume them in ways that suited me. And what suited me varied by time and place. I need content that will work on all of my devices, and I needed content that would rely on an internet connection. We'll discuss all of these technology practicalities in Part Two of this book.

Business-to-consumer example

I'm looking at what I can do with my airline loyalty points, how the process works and where I might like to go. This process is as much about enjoying the process of looking at the destinations I could visit as it is about making any sort of practical plan.

As I work through this process I will make a number of steps that may include, but are not limited to:

- trying to log into my account online to see how many points I have;
- understanding the process of using the points to book flights;
- seeing how far the flights can take me and a list of available destinations, without having a destination in mind;
- understanding when flights are available;
- looking at the destinations, exploring holiday options and looking at the suitability for different types of travel (romantic, family etc);
- working out the most cost-effective way of using my points considering airport taxes and other charges.

On initial inspection, none of these steps need be mobile-only steps. But also bear in mind I said this was as much about fun as it was about practical planning, so this was most likely to be done, in what

Harvard Business Review calls 'me' time (*Harvard Business Review*, February 2013). Therefore, a lot, if not all, of this research would be done on a mobile device from my sofa. Nearly 30 per cent of all website visits to travel sites are now carried out on mobile devices (Digital Tourism Think Tank, 2013).

I give this example because, not only is it real, but with my particular airline of choice it turned out to be nearly impossible. The key point here is that it was essential to understand the motivation of my user journey, and that was to explore, to learn and to 'mock plan'. Let's take a look at some of the issues that got in the way of this process meeting my requirements:

- main site redirecting to mobile site with limited functionality;
- no ability to go back to main website easily;
- main website not designed to work on multiple devices;
- search options not suited to my user journey, ie being unsure of my final destination;
- no easy way to browse availability without browsing through page after page of dates;
- no further information or recommended sites on potential destinations;
- unclear guidance on travel options when travelling with family (I will not be popular if I'm sitting in business class sipping cocktails and waving back to my family in economy).

These aren't just technology issues. They had an app after all. They just hadn't thought through the different user journeys, and the process had been mapped to work with their booking system rather than the user's needs.

If this journey was embraced, any airline or holiday company I was engaging with would have the opportunity to engage me, reinforce their brand and give me inspiration for future travel. Even if it didn't lead to me booking there and then, by making the process easier they could improve my brand loyalty and potential word-of-mouth recommendations. Instead I'm writing in a book about how frustrating it was!

Local intent

I have so far left out mentioning the locally-based consumer. Not because it isn't important, but because it can be a distraction from the broader picture. If your business has any sort of location-based offering it can be immensely powerful, but this goes back to our concept of understanding the target audience's objectives and context, and then using mobile technologies to deliver the most appropriate solution.

According to Google, 94 per cent of smartphone users have carried out a local search (Mobile Playbook, 2012). If I am looking for a local hotel, my nearest bus stop, a nearby provider of power supplies for my brand of laptop and so on, this type of search is transformational to both the mobile user and potentially any business involved.

We'll explore mobile and retail, where local mobile use can have a huge impact, in the next chapter on integration. We'll also look at mobile search in depth in Part Two and how this fits in with the user journey.

Content marketing

Content marketing is often talked about when looking at an over-arching web strategy, but it's also well worth considering when you are thinking about your mobile marketing. Fundamentally, content marketing is about providing useful and engaging content that is suited to the user's journey. Generally, content marketing is about providing value beyond your direct product offering. If we go back to my example of selecting a hosting provider, a useful focus for content marketing would have been educating the user about web technologies.

In Table 2.2 we consider a few more examples:

TABLE 2.2   Ideas for content marketing themes

Type of company	Focus of content marketing
SEO agency	Digital marketing advice
White water rafting (aimed at teams)	Human resources
Alcoholic drink brand	Cocktail-making and recipes
Detergent	Family money-savings tips
Sportswear	Training tips
Business service	Thought leadership articles

Content marketing, value proposition and mobile

Content marketing allows us to bolster our value proposition through digital delivered content or services. Mobile specifically allows us to deliver content in a form that is most useful to the audience at the right time. More importantly, we have the opportunity to use mobile technologies creatively to deliver this value proposition via interaction.

Let's take our ideas for content marketing themes, and in Table 2.3 look at how they could be applied in an interactive way:

TABLE 2.3   Content marketing themes and mobile interaction ideas

Focus of content marketing	Interactive idea
Digital marketing advice	Campaign reporting tool
Human resources	Interactive HR guide with scenario planning
Cocktail-making and recipes	Interactive portable recipe book
Family money-savings tips	Coupons and location-based savings
Training tips	Training objective progress tracker
Thought leadership articles	Podcast/audio for learning on the move

All of these very simple ideas could be developed into something far more robust that would interactively reinforce a brand value proposition.

It's important to understand how this can be applied to organizations with completely different products or service offerings. A B2B service is generally a high involvement purchase. That is, you think carefully and do some research before buying. Buying confectionery on the other hand is generally a very low involvement purchase. You're unlikely to go online and compare chocolate bars before buying them! However, using digital delivered services and content marketing can help bolster value proposition and brand positioning in both cases.

The stages of the user journey

Google have invested a lot of time in investigating the user journey and trying to understand the different stages we go through when making buying decisions. Let's also be realistic here. Much of the research published by Google ends with conclusions about how their products can fulfil the requirements outlined in the research (and why not, they are a commercial organization). Putting aside commercial objectives for a moment, let's take a look at a piece of work that I think is particularly useful when trying to understand the mobile consumer.

Procter & Gamble's First Moment of Truth

We'll start by taking a step back in time to 2005. Procter & Gamble published their take on what they called 'First Moment of Truth' (FMOT). This was covered widely in the press and made a significant impact on their overall strategy as outlined in the annual report of 2006 (Procter & Gamble, 2006).

The idea of FMOT was that there was some sort of initial advertising push the consumer was exposed to (which is called the 'Stimulus' part of the journey in the models we are going to explore), but much of the actual decision-making process was actually influenced at the brief moment when the consumer was at the shelf in the supermarket. Bear in mind that this model was originally targeted at what we'd call consumer packaged goods (CPG) or fast-moving consumer goods (FMCG), so it looked specifically at that set of potential user journeys.

They then speculated there was a 'Second Moment of Truth' (SMOT) when the customer purchased the product, took it home, used it and formed an opinion on it. These three steps of Stimulus, FMOT and SMOT made up the traditional wisdom of how to think about marketing campaigns.

Google's 'Zero Moment of Truth'

Some six years later Google decided this model was out of date and added one significant change to the model: the 'Zero Moment of Truth' (ZMOT). This is the step that comes between the Stimulus and the FMOT. It's when we do our research, educate ourselves, and compare and contrast products and services.

In a way, this is nothing new, as we always had word of mouth and asked the opinions of our trusted friends, colleagues and loved ones. What Google have suggested in this model is that the internet has enabled completely different consumer behaviour.

They then continued to prove this point by carrying out a series of research projects that looked at how much research people did before buying different types of products and how long they took to do this. The basic conclusion was that the ZMOT (see Figure 2.1) was now the most influential of what had become a four-step marketing model.

Limitations of ZMOT

The ZMOT model can be applied fairly widely, and in fact, in any scenario where some form of research is done online before purchase, it works pretty well. This could be a complex and fairly long buying cycle like a car or B2B service, or something more short term like comparing restaurant reviews online before visiting. What it doesn't work well for, though, are products like detergent or bread. In most cases we don't go online to research these types of products before purchase. However, if we expand our idea of the Zero Moment to include the kinds of interactive experiences we discussed earlier in this chapter, it can still be applied.

FIGURE 2.1   Google's Zero Moment of Truth (ZMOT) handbook

The feedback loop

Not only is this model interesting because it explores how the internet has changed our buying behaviour, but it also shows a much closer connection between our ZMOT, that point when we are researching online, and the SMOT, when we have experienced a product or service. It is easier than ever to leave reviews online that influence other consumers' buying decisions.

This feedback loop can be extremely powerful. For example, it has radically changed the travel industry with nearly 40 per cent of consumers consulting online reviews before booking (World Travel Market, January 2013).

This can be a mixed blessing for businesses. I was recently consulted by a large hotel group who asked me how to deal with a major problem that had arisen with numerous negative reviews on the TripAdvisor hotel review site. The answer, which I should say they gracefully took on board after some initial resistance, was that they needed to improve their hotels.

> You can get the full details on Google's Zero Moment of Truth by visiting: **www.zeromomentoftruth.com**.
>   Much of the research they started here is continued on their excellent Think with Google site: **www.thinkwithgoogle.com**.

Value proposition and user journey

Once we map out and understand our different target audiences, their different motivations and the user journeys they could potentially take, we start to have the basis of a digital plan. Once we align this to our business objectives and can measure for success and improvement we have the makings of a digital strategy.

The third and final section of this book will give you a series of checklists to help bring together your digital strategy.

CASE STUDY   PizzaExpress

Industry

Restaurant

Location

UK

Marketing objectives

Deliver meaningful improvements that directly responded to customer feedback. Improve sales and drive customer loyalty.

Their challenge

Following a customer survey, PizzaExpress identified one of their customers' biggest gripes was the time it took to wind up the dining experience and pay the bill. This was a particular issue for PizzaExpress as their customer base contains a large percentage of families, a market they have actively targeted. Once the meal was finished families struggled to keep young children entertained while waiting for their bill to arrive.

The two main insights from the survey were: 1) awareness of vouchers and offers available; and 2) the time it took to pay and leave once the meal was finished. As PizzaExpress is notoriously busy, having customers waiting to pay when other customers are waiting for tables was having an impact on sales as the third biggest concern was lack of available seating.

PizzaExpress wanted to respond to these specific issues by delivering a tangible improvement to the dining experience.

Their solution

PizzaExpress decided to develop a mobile app that would allow customers to not only book tables prior to their visit, but also pay their bill from their table and redeem any available voucher codes against their meal. They identified PayPal as their partner of choice for mobile payments due to its proven security and the level of customers already holding an existing account. The app was easy and simple to use for customers who could use it to pay their bill securely as soon as they had finished their meal, using a 12-digit code located at the bottom of their receipt. They had instant access to current voucher codes which could be applied to their bill at the point of checkout which saved customers having to research them and/or print out vouchers prior to their visit. This additional functionality increased the customer base as table booking and voucher codes could be accessed by customers who still preferred to pay their bill in person.

Once paid, confirmation was sent to both the customer and the restaurant till and the customer was free to leave.

The app went live in the summer of 2011 and has been updated regularly in response to customer feedback. It was the first of its kind to offer in-house online payments and the first collaboration of its kind for PayPal.

Their results

Within the first week the restaurant took more than £10,000 in payments through the app, rising to over £100,000 in the first month. The app also facilitated more than 15,000 booking requests, 5,000 more than the target set for the first month.

In addition, the app received worldwide coverage and PizzaExpress gained an additional 22,000 likes on its Facebook page.

Not only that, but the app improved efficiency in the restaurant as wait staff were spending less time dealing with payments.

What's good about it

The app was successful because it was designed to directly respond to what customers said they wanted. It's simple to use and doesn't require the customer to change their habits or behaviour in order to utilize it. PizzaExpress knows their target audience well and used customer insight to develop a tool which made a tangible difference to the customer experience.

The roll-out was well planned and involved a partnership programme to support high speed WiFi in all of their 400 restaurants in the UK.

It was the first app of its kind and the first time PayPal had been used in this way, which gained it additional coverage worldwide and supported brand awareness.

What they said about it

The creation of a PizzaExpress app was a clear opportunity for us to lead our sector with real innovation. We were determined that it shouldn't simply lead customers to their nearest restaurant and give them access to our menus, but improve their in-restaurant experience too. We were the first brand on the UK high street to allow our customers to pay using PayPal, as well as their credit or debit card. By introducing this functionality, and helping customers to settle their bill at any point during a meal, they are free to leave whenever they need to. It's proved particularly popular among parents with fidgety children.

Following the successful launch of our iPhone app we broadened our offering to the millions of Android users across the UK and took this opportunity to add a 'click and collect' function so customers can easily place takeaway orders. Our app continues to get a fantastic response from customers and is an important platform for customer interaction.

Emma Woods, Marketing Director

Technology change and adoption

As I have already said, mobile marketing is more about the user journey than it is about the technology. However, we need to understand the adoption of the technology to really understand our target audiences and how we can best reach them. In this chapter we will try and explore and benchmark where the technology currently fits into this puzzle and start to understand the differences between distinct markets and segments of our audience.

Forty years of radical change

At the time of writing it is 40 years to the day since Martin Cooper, a senior engineer at Motorola, made the first mobile phone call on 3 April 1973. Within 10 years they had launched the DynaTAX 8000x (Figure 3.1), their first commercial handheld mobile phone.

The change in the world of technology and how this has impacted the world of mobile has been radical to say the least. Bear in mind there was no internet when this phone was first in use and that SMS (short messaging service or 'text messaging' as it is often referred to) didn't even get a technical definition until some years later.

In 2012 a report carried out by the International Telecommunication Union found that there were six billion mobile phone subscriptions worldwide.

The global population at the time was seven billion.

FIGURE 3.1   The DynaTax 8000x: a snip at $3,995 in 1983!

Integrated devices

Our expectations of mobile devices are radically different now and smartphones and tablets offer us fully integrated computing and telecommunications devices. This integration is what has led to the radical change in usage that we need to understand in order to make the best use of mobile marketing.

When you consider the level of internet searches done on mobile devices, social media interactions and e-mail reading and writing (all of which we will explore shortly), we quickly see that the device becomes less and less relevant, whilst what we are doing with it becomes far more important.

Multi-platform consumption is today's new reality. One in three minutes spent online is now spent beyond the PC.

SOURCE: Mobile Future in Focus Report, 2013

Smartphone adoption

We could at this point start to look at dozens of charts and facts that wow us with the high level of adoption of mobile phone and smartphone technology (and forgive me, I will do this a little!). In reality though, smartphone adoption, as a percentage of population, is probably lower than most of us expect (Figure 3.2).

So, if smartphone penetration is actually below 50 per cent, even in highly developed markets like Asia (and even within Asia there are radical variations between regions) why are we getting so excited? Does this mean that this is a minority audience? The answer is actually no.

When you factor in some key demographic data like age, you start to realize that a large percentage of the population is unlikely to own smartphones in the first place. By this I mean young children. According to Index Mundi (who compile their data from the CIA *World Factbook* no less!), in February 2013 around 26.2 per cent of the world population was 0–14 years old. Many of this group are unlikely to own a smartphone. However, we will explore this further later, as for example, my 11-year-old daughter is a highly active smartphone user.

FIGURE 3.2 Smartphone adoption as a percentage of population

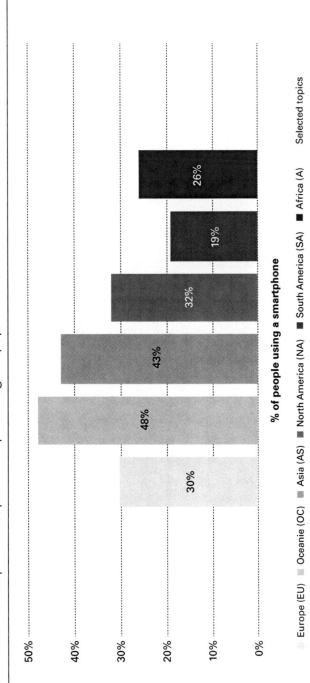

% of people using a smartphone

Europe (EU) ▪ Oceanie (OC) ▪ Asia (AS) ▪ North America (NA) ▪ South America (SA) ▪ Africa (A)   Selected topics

SOURCE: ConsumerBarometer.com, April 2013

FIGURE 3.3   Smartphone penetration variations

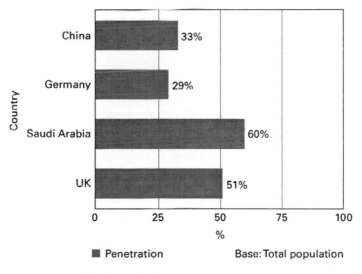

SOURCE: Our Mobile Planet, 2012

Global variations

We also need to be careful to understand the global variations in smartphone adoption and what is causing this (Figure 3.3).

Many of these variations in adoption rates are related to income (smartphones tend to be more expensive than basic 'feature phones') and geographical coverage offered by the various mobile phone operators that offer data connections.

For example, currently the three major phone operators in China on average have only 22 per cent 3G data penetration (*Forbes*, February 2013). This is, however, skewed by the fact that China Mobile, the largest mobile operator in China, has only 13 per cent 3G penetration. However, with China Mobile due to launch the latest iPhone on their network imminently (the first time they have offered the iPhone) this is expected to change very quickly.

This is in contrast to the UK market where figures from Informa (MobiThinking, December 2012) show over 77 per cent of the population are using 3G data. Although German smartphone penetration is low in relation to many parts of Europe, it is growing most quickly for this region (eMarketer, April 2013).

Similar figures looking at data usage and availability in Saudi Arabia show over 90 per cent 3G penetration (Our Mobile World, December 2012).

Benchmarking marketing activity

These regional differences in smartphone usage go much deeper than just adoption. We need to understand how users are actually using their mobile devices. For example, Figure 3.4 shows that mobile search (that is, using a search engine via a mobile device) has seen over 1,000 per cent growth on Baidu (China's largest search engine) in the two years between 2010 and the beginning of 2013.

A great example of the differences between countries is when we look at the percentage of smartphone users that actually use their device to browse the web. It varies from 15 per cent in India through to 80 per cent in South Korea (Nielsen, *The Mobile Consumer*, 2013).

Listing all of the variations across the globe would not be practical in a book of this type (and wouldn't make for very exciting reading!), so instead of trying to do this, I'd like to highlight some tools that will help you work out what is relevant for your market.

Our Mobile Planet: http://www.thinkwithgoogle.com/mobileplanet/

This is a great tool that has been updated annually since 2011. It allows you to look at a variety of mobile statistics including adoption and behaviour for a wide range of global markets. The data behind it were compiled by Google, IAB, Ipsos and the Mobile Marketing Association.

You can isolate a particular country and behaviour or compare and contrast by building your own charts.

An easy-to-miss feature is that you can download a report and/or the full data for any particular country by using the 'Dive Deeper into the Data' feature you'll find on the home page (Figure 3.5).

Bear in mind that one limitation of the data is that it is purely for smartphones and doesn't include mobile devices at this stage.

FIGURE 3.4 Baidu: growth in mobile search 2010–2013

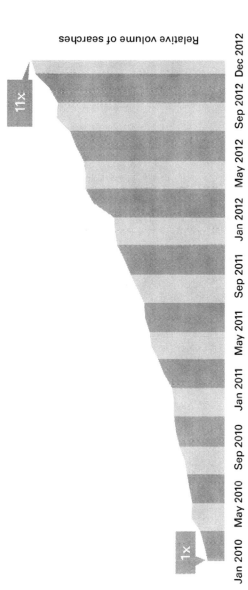

Relative volume of searches

11x

1x

Jan 2010   May 2010   Sep 2010   Jan 2011   May 2011   Sep 2011   Jan 2012   May 2012   Sep 2012   Dec 2012

TechInAsia, February 2013

FIGURE 3.5   Our Mobile Planet tool (www.consumerbarometer.com)

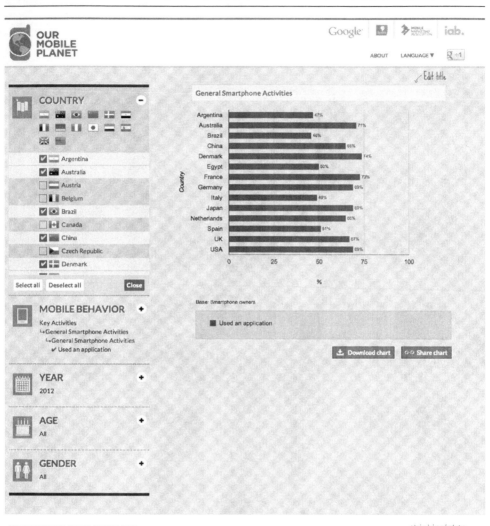

DIVE DEEPER INTO THE DATA

 Download the full data set by country and learn about the state of mobile with country level reports from the 2012 Our Mobile Planet Smartphone Research.

Download Now ▶

thinkinsights
with Google

Consumer Barometer

Although the Consumer Barometer is not purely a mobile marketing tool, it is excellent for understanding how mobile makes up part of the overall user journey.

The tool highlights data from 39 countries and looks at how people use the internet to research and buy products (see Figure 3.6). You can explore the data by browsing around, or by building your own charts as with the Mobile Planet tool.

FIGURE 3.6   Consumer Barometer tool (www.consumerbarometer.com)

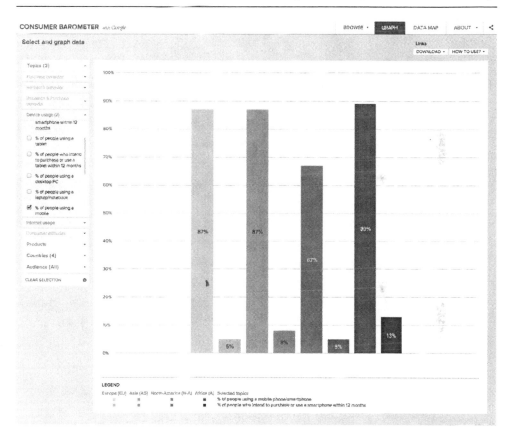

For a list of the latest mobile marketing tools and market insights visit:
http://www.targetinternet.com/mobilemarketing.

04 Disruption and integration

We have so far examined the mobile consumer and some of the high level technology issues that have impacted the broad world of mobile marketing. What we haven't done is look in a little more detail at the profound and disruptive effect mobile is already having on some businesses and markets.

Much of this change comes back to our understanding of the user journey, but really it is about convenience, choice and transparency of information for the consumer.

My favourite statistic to demonstrate this is that 87 per cent of retailers believe that shoppers can find better deals via their mobile device (Motorola Solutions, Annual Holiday Survey, 2012). In the same report, it's believed that 39 per cent of walkouts (when a consumer leaves a store without purchasing) were influenced by mobile phone usage.

> 87 per cent of retailers believe that shoppers can find better deals via their mobile device.

This is crazy. If we know that people aren't buying because of price, and that they can easily find out that lower prices are available elsewhere, we have a few simple choices. We can compete on price (very difficult in retail), find something else to compete on (like service, quality of experience, value added etc), or get out of the business before it fails. Painful news for many retailers but true none the less.

This fundamental shift in what retailers need to provide has been caused by the convenience, choice and transparency that mobile, and more broadly, digital marketing gives.

The attitude of many retailers is that if you need something urgently you will still come into the store. This is also being disrupted by digital and smart business. I needed to buy an audio cable for my computer. I knew that my best chance locally was a store called Maplin who always stocked these kinds of products. Not only was the website able to tell me if they had the correct cable in stock, in what stores and how many, they also had smart delivery options. I could get it next day, but more importantly I could get it delivered to my home within 90 minutes (using a smart service called Shutl). Bearing in mind this was cheaper than paying for parking near the store, why would I go in-store?

The death of in-store retail

So does this mean that retail is dead? No, but it means it needs to change and adapt to an environment that has radically changed. People will still go in-store, but for different reasons. It may be for the excellent product advice, great experience, to get hands-on with a product or as a leisure activity. The one thing you can be sure of though is that, if you are competing on price, in-store retail is going to be increasingly challenging, unless your store acts as part of a multi-channel approach.

Mobile: the saviour of retail

There is however an alternative view to this scenario. It still includes radical change, but envisions mobile as the saviour of in-store retail. Let's consider the concept that we explored in Chapter 2, of using mobile technology to create experiences that bolster the value proposition. There is no reason that mobile can't bolster the value proposition that it's worth going in-store.

By utilizing the appropriate technology, be it apps, near field communication (NFC) or mobile-optimized websites (all of which we'll explore in Part Two), we can improve the in-store retail experience

It may just be that the store experience drives the online sale, but if that is the case we need to understand the user journey to analyse this.

Mobile search can tell me that another online retailer is selling the same product I'm looking at in-store cheaper online. However, it can also tell me that the store I'm in offers better quality customer service post-sale, a great returns policy and free in-store product training. It may be that by buying in-store I get access to a loyalty programme, or because I've signed up to their app/website I get priority treatment in-store.

For years airlines and hotels have used loyalty programmes to attract repeat custom from a market that may otherwise be price sensitive. Many of the same principles can be applied to mobile and retail (and many other markets as well).

Convenience, choice and transparency

When we look at markets that have been disrupted by digital technology, the key is to understand why this technology has changed the user experience and journey (or context of the journey).

The media industry has been massively disrupted. Music, film and publishing have all seen massive changes in the delivery of their product. Technology has created a more convenient, flexible and instantaneous delivery channel than ordering a physical product. While there will always be a demand for vinyl and print, the increased convenience, choice and the transparency of pricing meant that the industry changed quickly and consumers moved more quickly than media companies. The user experience had changed, massively for the better, and instead of embracing this, the industry dragged their heels. This allowed online piracy to seem like a viable alternative to many who would have paid online, given the option. Over 65 per cent of people are now willing to pay for content online (Nielsen, 2013).

Business culture

This brings us to a highly important point: that of the culture within an organization. In a fast paced, rapidly changing environment, which digital and mobile will continue to be for the foreseeable future, we need a culture that allows for change and flexibility. The technology behind mobile marketing in itself is not too complex (or at least I hope you'll think so by the time you read Part Two of this book).

What is complex and generally difficult is change within organizations. Change management has always been challenging, and what mobile marketing is causing is the need for ongoing change. We need to build organizations and organizational culture that allows for rapid change. In my experience, the bigger the company, the harder this can be.

Single customer view

One very practical aspect of this is the ability to understand our potential and existing customers better. We have access to more data than ever before (we'll explore this data from mobile apps, advertising and websites in Part Two). As we collect more and more data though, we need to actually do something with it. It needs to be analysed and actions taken.

Doing something with data

In my experience many companies are now collecting and reporting on web analytics data. What they are not doing is analysing that data in any robust way and actioning that analysis. There is quite often a monthly meeting where a couple of charts are shown, generally looking at volume-based data like number of site visits. The chart is going up, everyone looks happy and the meeting moves on.

This is a huge missed opportunity to learn and improve our digital marketing efforts; data can give us great insight into how effective our mobile marketing is actually being. Take a look at Chapter 18 on mobile analytics to learn more about this.

The idea of a single customer view is a very simple one, but can be extremely difficult to achieve (particularly in larger organizations). The idea is that we connect up the data we get from our mobile apps, websites, e-mail campaigns, social media and so on, build a complete picture of our audience, and are thus able to become smarter marketers. In the best-case scenario, we can connect all of this data to our customer relationship management (CRM) systems and we have a unified and easy way to interrogate sources of information.

FIGURE 4.1   Achieving a single customer view

The painful truth about integration

The challenge of integrating data sources is that it is generally a fairly complicated IT project for most organizations. What we are really talking about is database, third-party supplier and legacy systems integration, and what this means in reality is complexity. However, it doesn't need to be this way.

If I am a small business, it's a different picture. I can get some form of web analytics like Google Analytics, a cloud-based CRM system like Salesforce, and various systems like MailChimp (an online e-mail service provider (ESP)). All of these will 'plug in' to one another with not too much effort, and I have a relatively effective single customer view.

Even in large organizations, by carefully selecting suppliers with a single customer view in mind, I can work toward this ideal scenario step by step. We may not be able to integrate all data immediately, but this should be our long-term objective.

Next step: marketing automation

Marketing automation is something that is most often used in the B2B world, but it can be applied to almost any industry, product or service to some extent. The core principle is that if I have insight into your behaviour on a single or multiple channels, I can automatically trigger relevant communications to you at the right time.

At its most simple level, imagine getting a push notification via an app some time after you have made a purchase, asking for a review. This is a basic form of marketing automation.

At its more advanced level I can start to 'score' your behaviour across multiple platforms to try and identify particular types of customers, potential leads or customers who are having problems finding the right information.

The B2B world tends to be well suited to marketing automation due to the long sales times, involved buying process, multiple touch points before purchase and high value of a sale. It can also be applied to consumer goods if tied in with digital services that are there to bolster value proposition. For example, a sportswear manufacturer can track your behaviour through an app that monitors your fitness goals and triggers relevant communications at the right time.

Mobile as a change enabler

So we've looked at how mobile technology can be disruptive, but also how this can actually be a change for good by improving the customer experience and can lead to improved awareness, engagement and loyalty in the long term. By fully exploiting the technology available in a way that embraces the increased convenience, choice and transparency available to the mobile consumer, we can mitigate risk and maximize opportunity.

CASE STUDY   Tesco

Industry

Retail

Location

Korea

Marketing objectives

- Increase customer numbers both in-store and online.

- Become the number 1 supermarket in Korea without increasing the number of stores.

Their challenge

Tesco (Homeplus as it's known in Korea) is the second biggest supermarket in the Korean market, surpassed only by E-mart who own a significantly larger number of stores.

Koreans are one of the hardest working nations in the world and the weekly grocery shop is seen as an arduous task that is something to endure.

So Tesco started thinking about ways they could drive customers to their online store by providing an easy alternative to shopping in-store, fitting in with Koreans' busy lives and appealing to their desire to avoid the supermarket altogether.

Their solution

Tesco worked with marketing and communications agency Cheil Worldwide to design and install a virtual store in Korea's subways. The walls were made up to look like the aisles in the supermarket with each product and variation thereof occupying the same space as it would in-store.

Alongside each product was a UR code that, once scanned, would drop the corresponding product directly into a virtual trolley. Once the shopping had been finalized and paid for, the groceries were delivered to the customer's home on the same day.

Their results

Between November 2010 and January 2011, 10,287 customers visited the online store via their smartphones. The number of new sign-ups to their online shopping rose by 76 per cent and sales rose by a massive 130 per cent.

The campaign cemented Tesco as the number 1 online grocery retailer in Korea and a very close second overall despite having far fewer physical stores than the market leader.

What's good about it

Tesco is well known for adapting their brand to the local community, even changing from store to store within the same county. And the success of this campaign was based largely on their insight into the wider culture, not just shopping habits.

Tesco really got to grips with what makes their customers tick and delivered an experience that went beyond gimmick to something that made a real difference to customers' day-to-day lives.

What they said about it

It gives us a unique window into the future and the chance to try out exciting new concepts.

The virtual store blends clicks and bricks, bringing together our love of browsing with the convenience of online shopping.

We think this concept can work outside of Korea, since many young people around the world are adopting smartphone technology.

Jo Hyun Jae, Homeplus Project Co-ordinator

05 Devices, platforms and technology: why it doesn't matter

It's easy to get bogged down in working out which mobile devices your app should work on, what happens when a new phone version comes out and how effective your responsive design website is (all of which we explore in detail in Part Two). All of this stuff matters because of the final outcome of your mobile campaigns, but the reality is that your mobile consumers don't care. They just want to be able to get stuff done.

Responsive design means absolutely nothing to the majority of the people on this planet (and maybe to you right now) and nor should it. I don't really care how my house was built as long as it keeps me dry, warm and secure. However, if my house doesn't work when it rains, or when the sun shines, I will have a serious problem with the builders.

You need to worry about the technical aspects of your mobile strategy but your users should not. They shouldn't even notice it.

Mobile-compatible is not mobile-optimized

Just because your website works on mobile devices does not mean it is mobile optimized. What I mean is that the site may load up fine on my phone, but if I have to zoom in a dozen times to see anything clearly, this isn't an optimal experience.

We'll explore the ins and outs of building mobile sites in Part Two, but what we need to consider now is what my target audience is likely to do, in what context and on what devices. I can then start to make sure I have ticked the appropriate boxes to make their experience as pain-free as possible.

Users are even more impatient on mobile devices than they are when using a desktop or laptop (KissMetrics, 2013). They have come across so many poor mobile sites they just give up very quickly. On the other hand, if we can create a seamless mobile experience we stand a better chance of achieving our objectives and can actually build loyalty.

Technology challenges

So, you're thinking something along the lines of 'It's all very good saying the technology doesn't matter, but I have to make choices and every time I make a change it costs money'. You're 100 per cent right. The reality is this has always been the case in marketing. We have to decide where to spend our money and how to prioritize our budgets. The actual problem here is that the number of options is large and we don't ask the right questions.

Asking the right questions

Rather than asking whether you should build an Android, iOS or a Blackberry app (if you have no idea what I'm talking about, take a look at the box below), we should actually be asking what devices your target audience uses and which groups will it be most cost effective to reach. Let's frame this for a moment by forgetting about mobile. If I decide I am targeting an audience but can only afford to target half of it, I need to decide which half. I don't do this based on an opinion; I should most likely do it on the potential lifetime value of those customers, how much it will cost to target them and other commercially focused criteria. The same applies to the different mobile platforms and choices we make within our mobile strategies.

Platform wars

We'll explore the technical side of mobile sites and apps in Part Two, but it's worth understanding the key players in the mobile operating system (OS) market. For the sake of simplicity we've just looked at the major smartphone and tablet platforms here. An OS is just the software that a phone runs on and will impact its functionality. Most importantly for us, apps built for one platform, generally don't work on another. We'll look at these in more detail later.

Android

Google's mobile OS. It's open source, meaning it can theoretically be used and adapted by anyone. It has also been adopted by the Open Handset Alliance (OHA) which includes big handset manufacturers such as Samsung, Sony and HTC.

iOS

Apple's OS, used on its iPhone, iPod, AppleTV and iPad products range. It is closely associated with OS X used on Apple Mac computers.

Blackberry

Blackberry's OS for all Blackberry devices.

Windows Phone

Microsoft's OS is used by several handset manufacturers, including Nokia on their Lumia range of phones. It is not compatible with Windows for PCs.

Beyond these platforms with the largest market share there are a whole lot more. Take a look at Wikipedia to see just how many – and then don't worry about them! (By the way, if you are going to send me hate mail about telling people to ignore your particular mobile OS of choice, you should probably get out more.) **http://wikipedia.org/wiki/Mobile_operating_system**.

Audience segmentation

Just because 40 per cent of the world uses a particular type of mobile OS, it doesn't mean that your target audience in your target market does. For this reason you shouldn't rely on a lot of the generalized statistics that are published. If you do need some initial guidance, take a look at the next chapter that tries to summarize the key trends and statistics from each region of the world.

In reality, your target audience probably won't align with the norms of your particular market, and if you're working across multiple regions it clearly gets more complicated. What we really need to do is to collect some actual market insights as we should with any other aspect of our marketing. You can do this by sample surveying your target audience and actually asking the question.

Frictionless technology

What we are aiming for is to make the process of achieving the consumer's goal as simple and as transparent as possible. This idea of making the process as seamless as possible is often referred to as 'frictionless technology' and it's something we'll consider throughout Part Two of this book. What we should be always consider in our mobile marketing is what is the objective of the user and how can that most effectively be achieved using the right technology in the right place.

CASE STUDY   Catalina and ExactTarget

Industry

Retail, Consumer Packaged Goods

Location

Europe, Japan, Europe

Marketing objectives

Catalina serves clients with behaviour-based marketing and targeted advertising campaigns. Partnering with retailers and manufacturers of consumer packaged goods (CPG), Catalina uses transactional data, including frequent shopper card information, obtained at point-of-sale, to provide relevant CPG coupons to shoppers.

ExactTarget is a data-driven digital marketing company.

Their challenge

Use customer data and mobile technologies to drive in-store visits and increase sales.

Their solution

Catalina's extensive understanding and experience with shopper data, coupled with an ExactTarget partnership resulted in 'targeted' e-mail and SMS campaigns. They co-branded with retailers and created 'yourbucks,' powered by Catalina's Coupon Network platform. Catalina provided an avenue for shoppers to digitally opt in to their current programmes. 'Partnered with retailers, we capture shoppers interested in a mobile and e-mail club by following the same processes used to develop our point-of-sale programmes,' says Matthew Lee, Director of Digital Product Marketing. Catalina created and hosted registration sites for each retailer, branded to look like the retailer's own website. At each site, customers are asked if they want to participate in the e-mail or text couponing programmes.

In addition, Catalina uses ExactTarget Mobile for SMS messaging. By texting a keyword (ie 'SHOP') and their frequent shopper card number to a short code, consumers are opted-in to an SMS programme for additional communications. Coupon distribution is based on targeting criteria, like previous shopping experiences, making it easy to reach each consumer with relevant marketing campaigns and positively impacting their clients' return on investment (ROI). 'For example, we may send an e-mail or text including a major brand diaper offer to folks who have purchased diapers. Retailers love it because it provides relevant coupons for their shoppers from major brands, and it drives the shopper back to their store,' says Lee.

Their results

Retailers received proven results by participating in the 'yourbucks' programme, including:

- 18.9 per cent increase in in-store visits;
- 24.3 per cent increase in average spend per trip;
- 7 per cent increase in margins for promoted products.

What's good about it

It uses a combination of technologies, integrated with powerful data in order to drive very significant results. It seamlessly fits into the user journey and makes use of appropriate technology, data and communications at the appropriate time.

What they said about it

We built this digital marketing solution to drive significant results for our retail partners by providing value that matters to each consumer.

Matthew Lee, Director of Digital Product Marketing, Catalina

06 Mobile statistics summary

In this brief chapter we have compiled some of the latest statistics in what is an extremely fast moving and fragmented environment. We've taken a look at some of the key trends in global mobile marketing and brought together some data from a host of sources. You can see the full set of sources we used at the back of this book, but we've also highlighted some of the resources we think you will find most useful.

The fast paced nature of the environment means that the numbers reported on here will change rapidly. For this reason we've also provided an online resource that will give you the latest data and trends.

All the latest mobile marketing news and statistics

You can get all of the latest statistics, along with mobile marketing news and opinions by visiting the link: **http://www.targetinternet.com/mobilemarketing/**.

Breakdown of regions

Many of the statistics reported on here are broken down into fairly large regions. We have tried to separate out individual countries or smaller regions that show significant differences from the rest of the geographic region (for example, the USA is separated from the rest of North America to demonstrate the variations in statistics), but bear in mind this may be due to limitations of the currently available data in some cases. You should also remember that even within a particular region there can be significant regional variations. This is especially true of the Asia region, and for this reason we have provided further online resources for the most detailed and up-to-date data.

Smartphone adoption levels

We have already taken a look at the levels of smartphone adoption as a percentage of population in Chapter 3. Adoption levels of around 50 per cent (as a percentage of population) are the highest, seen in Asia and North America. In other areas that figure is much lower. Eastern Europe has the one of the lowest adoption rates of only 7 per cent, followed by Africa at 19 per cent.

These statistics represent some of the fastest changing numbers in this section, so check our online data for the latest numbers.

Mobile broadband subscriptions

The graph in Figure 6.1 shows the percentage of all smartphone/ tablet users who subscribe to mobile broadband. This basically means they have access to data services as part of their mobile phone subscription. Japan is top of the list with 80 per cent of all mobile subscriptions having broadband capacity, closely followed by North America at 79 per cent and Asia and Eastern Europe joint 3rd with 72 per cent. Within the Asia region South Korea is significantly ahead of the rest of the region with around 79 per cent as well.

Breakdown of mobile operating systems worldwide

Looking at mobile OS across the world (see Figure 6.2) we can immediately see the difference is usage between developed and developing countries and regions. Android and iOS come out on top for the

FIGURE 6.1 Mobile broadband subscription as a percentage of smartphone/tablet users

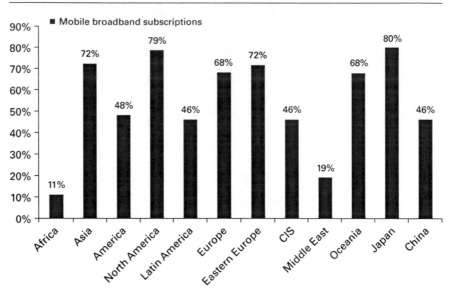

SOURCE: StatCounter

western world, whereas Windows and Symbian OS are more prevalent in developing areas.

Europe and Japan are the only two areas to show a fairly even split between Android and iOS, whereas in all other regions this split is far more significant.

The Symbian OS is most prevalent in Africa where 19 per cent of all phones use this operating system compared with only 7 per cent using iOS. As the data covers the whole continent, this can slightly skew the perspective, taking into account the smaller, more densely populated areas in South Africa where the majority of Blackberry and iOS users are located.

For iOS the highest percentage of user adoption is in Australia with the United States and Europe close behind.

In the rest of Oceania and Japan, Android and iOS are the only significant systems in use with Blackberry taking up only a small percentage of users across the region.

FIGURE 6.2 Mobile operating systems adoption worldwide

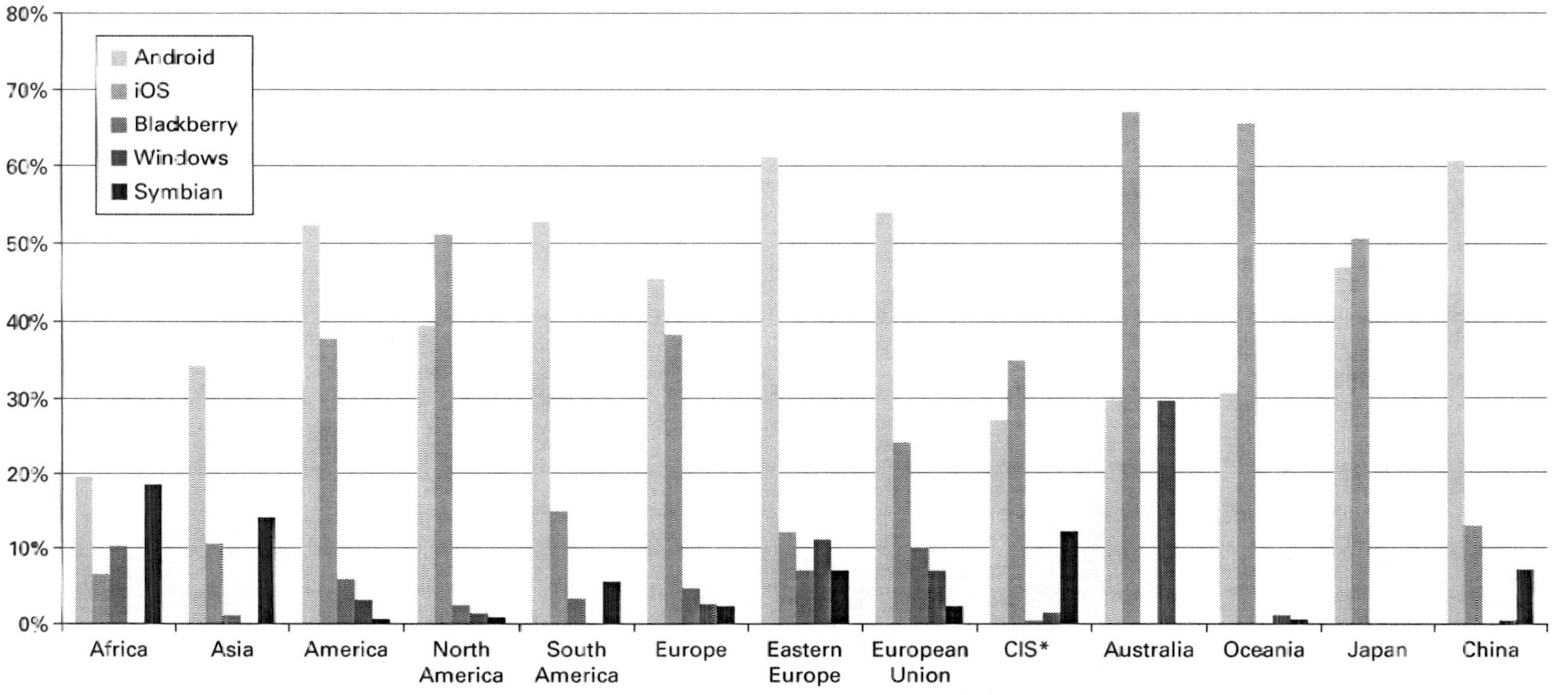

SOURCE: StatCounter

* Commonwealth of Independent States

In Figures 6.3 to 6.15 below, wherever a platform is not represented in the chart, it is generally the case that there is some adoption,
but it is too low to be statistically significant (this is why the charts
do not add up to exactly 100 per cent in some cases).

Mobile operating systems adoption by world region

FIGURE 6.3   Africa

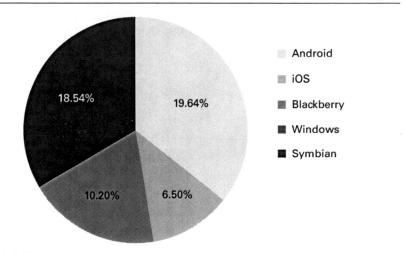

Android
iOS
Blackberry
Windows
Symbian

SOURCE: StatCounter

FIGURE 6.4   Asia

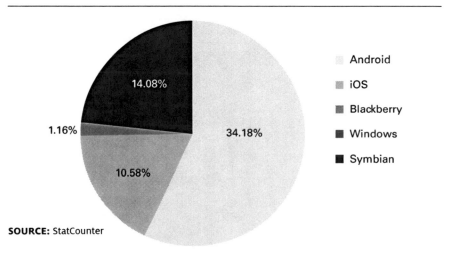

Android
iOS
Blackberry
Windows
Symbian

SOURCE: StatCounter

FIGURE 6.5   United States of America

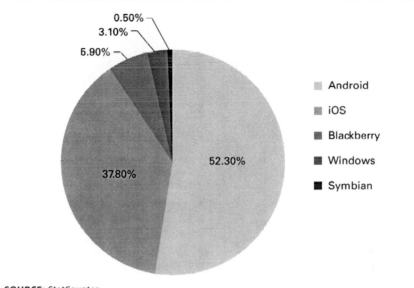

0.50%
3.10%
5.90%

Android
iOS
Blackberry
Windows
Symbian

52.30%
37.80%

SOURCE: StatCounter

FIGURE 6.6   North America

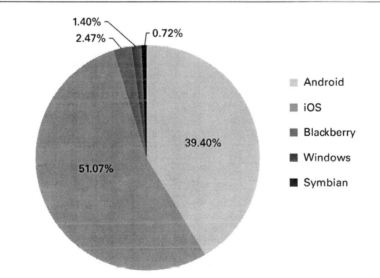

1.40%
2.47%
0.72%

Android
iOS
Blackberry
Windows
Symbian

39.40%
51.07%

SOURCE: StatCounter

FIGURE 6.7 South America

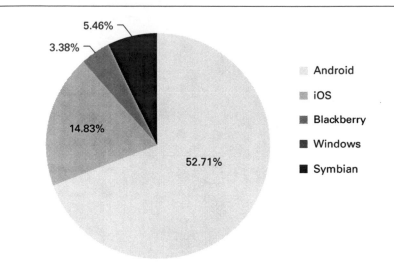

SOURCE: StatCounter

FIGURE 6.8 Europe

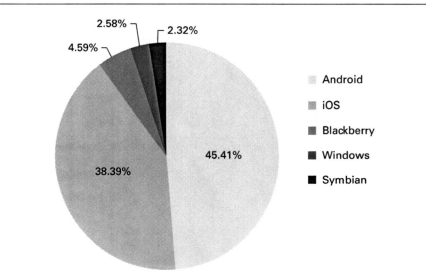

SOURCE: StatCounter

FIGURE 6.9   Eastern Europe

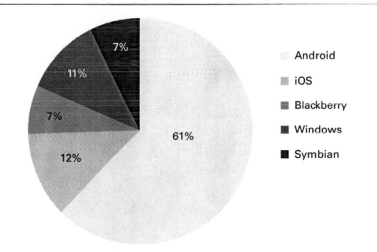

SOURCE: StatCounter

FIGURE 6.10   European Union

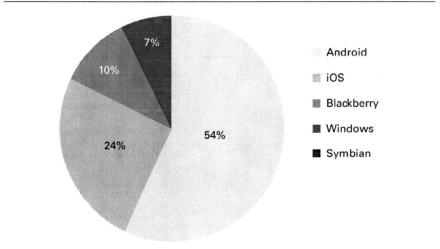

SOURCE: StatCounter

FIGURE 6.11   Commonwealth of Independent States (CIS)

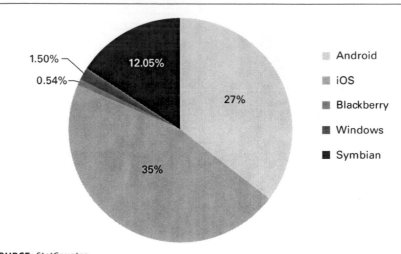

SOURCE: StatCounter

FIGURE 6.12   Australia

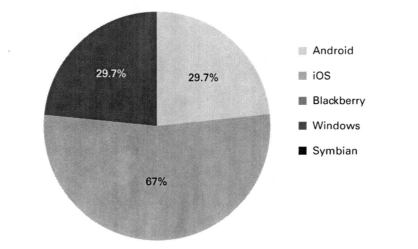

SOURCE: StatCounter

FIGURE 6.13   Oceania

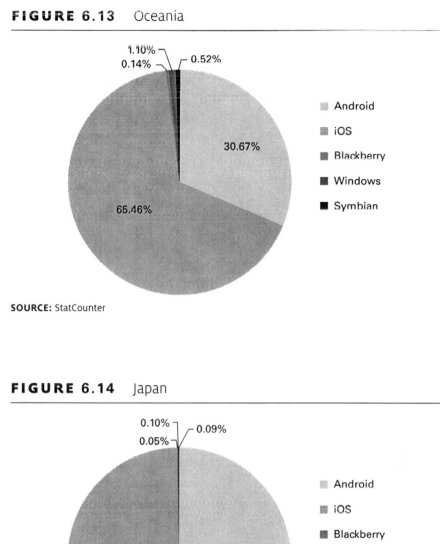

1.10%
0.14%   0.52%

30.67%

65.46%

Android
iOS
Blackberry
Windows
Symbian

SOURCE: StatCounter

FIGURE 6.14   Japan

0.10%   0.09%
0.05%

50.61%   46.89%

Android
iOS
Blackberry
Windows
Symbian

SOURCE: StatCounter

FIGURE 6.15 China

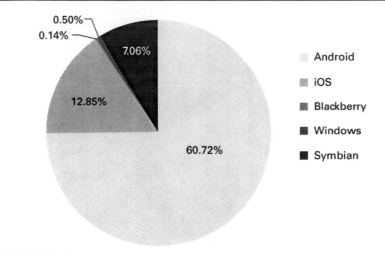

SOURCE: StatCounter

QR codes, NFC and other technologies

We'll explore each of the mobile technologies in more detail in Part Two of this book, but it's worth highlighting a couple of key issues at this stage.

The main issue is one of massively fragmented data and no absolutely clear picture. For example, figures on the use of QR (quick response) codes are pretty patchy to say the least. Most statistics show usage rates dramatically increasing with some markets showing growth rates in the thousands of per cent! However, we also need to bear in mind what the starting numbers were that delivered these growth rates. Growing by 10,000 per cent is impressive, but less impressive if the starting number was 0.00001 per cent of the population!

The other considerations are that the overall use of a particular technology in a particular region varies widely, impacted by things like demographics and job role.

However, probably the most important point here is how effectively these technologies are woven into a digital strategy. The usage of these types of technology can vary from statistical averages when used in a compelling and effective way. Take a look at some of the case studies and examples in Part Two for more evidence of this.

When it comes to demographics, we know that men are far more likely to scan QR codes or use NFC than women, and that more than half of all users are in the 18–35 age group (Pitney Bowes, *QR Code Adoption*, 2013).

Almost half of all QR codes are scanned at home either in magazines/newspapers or on consumable products and around one third of those codes link directly to a website or promotion page (eMarketer, *QR Code Usage*, 2013).

Take a look at Part Two for more detail on each specific technology.

Mobile social media usage by region

Looking at the spread of social media usage on mobile, Facebook comes out way ahead for all regions except the CIS and China. YouTube is a close second for mobile access. According to YouTube statistics, 25 per cent of all YouTube videos are accessed through mobile devices and there are more than 1 billion views on YouTube every day via mobile.

Chinese social media market

It's worth noting at this point that the Chinese market is significantly different to the rest of the world in regard to social media and mobile search. Many of the channels used globally such as Facebook, Twitter and YouTube are not available in China due to government filtering of the internet. This has led to a fast paced and highly innovative internal market served by market-leading companies like Tencent, Sina and Baidu. Because of the way data is collected globally to understand social usage, it means that data from the Chinese market is not always accurate on a like-for-like basis. We'll explore mobile social media and search usage more in Part Two, but you can see the main players in the figures below.

Social media usage by region data

Table 6.1 gives the breakdown of social media usage from mobile devices by world region:

TABLE 6.1 Social media usage by world region, 2013

%	YouTube	Facebook	Twitter	LinkedIn	Stumble Upon	Pinterest	Reddit	Orkut	VKontakte	Odnoklassniki	Other
Africa	6.52	**88.58**	2.03	0.29	1.14	0.93	0.25	–	–	–	0.26
Asia	11.84	**78.41**	5.92	0.45	1.16	–	0.43	–	–	–	1.79
Japan	9.33	**50.15**	29.74	0.25	2.86	–	2.55	–	–	–	5.12
USA	7.55	**47.38**	4.67	0.31	14.16	–	5.96	–	–	–	19.97
North America	7.49	**48.87**	5.39	0.3	13.76	17.63	5.85	–	–	–	0.71
South America	8.93	**80.57**	7.87	0.11	1.06	0.89	0.25	0.16	–	–	0.16
Europe	6.34	**77.08**	6.4	0.32	3.7	1.75	2.1	–	1.54	–	0.77
CIS	7.4	15.62	7.26	0.2	1.27	1.53	1.04	–	**60.18**	4.83	0.67
Oceania	7.06	**63.23**	5.38	0.43	9.76	–	6.74	–	–	–	7.4

SOURCE: StatCounter, 2013

Mobile marketing statistics

We have used a very wide range of sources for this section (all listed at the back of this book). This has been due mainly to the fragmented nature of the data available. However, we have found a number of sources and websites invaluable when researching this section and many other areas of this book. For this reason I've included some of the key ones here that I think will also be helpful to you:

StatCounter

http://gs.statcounter.com
Fantastic source of mobile, and lots of other web data that is available for use on a Creative Commons Licence. (This means you need to credit that the data came from StatCounter and give a link back to their website.)

MobiThinking

http://www.mobithinking.com
As well as publishing huge amounts of content on mobile marketing, MobiThinking is excellent at compiling and publishing the latest global data from a vast array of sources.

Target Internet

http://www.targetinternet.com/mobilemarketing/
Let's be clear, this is my website! However, I've pulled together all of the sources I've used for this book into one place, along with a load of other resources I think you'll find useful.

07 The future of mobile marketing

No book on mobile would be complete without considering the future of the technology and industry. My main thoughts on this are that the future is a lot closer than we think!

Exponential development

One of the main drivers in the development of mobile marketing is the exponential growth of computing power. As computing power increases and devices get physically smaller, so what our mobile devices can do becomes more and more interesting. Advances like voice recognition, augmented reality (AR) and high-resolution video displays have all relied on these increases in computing power to make them available on mainstream mobile devices.

Enter Moore's Law

Moore's Law is an often quoted, but quite often not fully understood, observation in regard to the exponential growth of computing power made back in 1965. Gordon E Moore, co-founder of Intel, observed that the number of transistors on integrated circuits doubled roughly every two years.

These changes have a direct impact on the speed at which computers can process information, how much storage they can have in a given space, and are even connected to things like the potential resolution of your digital camera.

This means that computing power grows at an exponential rate (more on that later).

Moore's Law has proved to be exceptionally accurate; although he originally predicted that it would hold true for around 10 years, it has now done so for nearly 50 years.

The future of Moore's Law

There has been much discussion about the fact that Moore's Law cannot continue to hold true forever. Practically speaking, you can only get so many transistors in a physical space before you get to the limit of what is possible due to the limitations of physics.

However, if you look at Moore's Law more broadly, and think in terms of computing power, rather than transistors, there is a clear argument in favour of it holding true. What generally happens, when one technology reaches the limits of what can be done with it, is that some form of innovation is found to continue the progress of technology. Whether that's an entirely new material, manufacturing process or brand new technology, there are lots of examples of innovation allowing Moore's Law to continue when it looked to be reaching its limits.

Exponential growth in perspective

One of the most important elements of this growth in computing power that is impacting our mobile devices is its exponential rate. The human brain is very good at understanding things that grow in a linear way, that is, something that grows at the same rate on an ongoing basis, like counting from 1 to 100. What we are not so good at is getting our heads around exponential growth. The best way to do this is to consider an example.

I first heard the following analogy from my friend, and expert digital strategist, Jonathan Macdonald (look up some of his talks for some real inspiration on the future of technology). I have seen a number of different versions of the analogy online, but the key thing is to take note at the end of the story.

Filling a stadium with water, one drop at a time

Imagine a large stadium filling with water from a tap, one drip per minute, and imagine that stadium to be watertight so that no water could escape. If the tap continued dripping water in the same regular (linear) way, it would take many thousands of years to fill the stadium.

However, if that tap was dripping at an exponential rate, so that the number of drips coming out of the tap doubled every minute, it's a very different story. The first minute there is one drop, the second minute there are two drops, the third minute four drops, the fourth minute eight drops and so on. This is exponential growth in action.

Now imagine you are sitting on the seat at the very top of the stadium, with a view across the entire area. The first drop from the exponential tap is dropped right in the middle of the stadium field, at 12 pm. Remembering that this drop grows exponentially by doubling in size every minute, how much time do you have to leave the stadium before the water reaches your seat at the very top? Is it hours, days, weeks, months or years?

The answer is that you have exactly until 12.49 pm. It takes an exponential tap less than 50 minutes to fill a whole stadium with water. This is impressive but it gets more interesting. At what time do you think the football stadium is still 93 per cent empty? The answer: at 12.45 pm. So if you sat and watched the water level growing, after 45 minutes all you would see is the stadium field covered with water. Then, within four more minutes, the water would fill the entire stadium. It would then take one more minute to fill an entire other stadium. Exponential growth gets very big, very quickly.

Technology as an enabler

So let's consider what this growth in technology means in practical terms. It means that the devices we use will be able to do more and more things that previously seemed impossible, and the rate of these technology developments will get faster and faster.

You only have to look at technology development over the few decades to see this in practice. Thirty years or so ago, my iPhone would have looked like science fiction. (It should be noted, however, I still don't have a hover car.)

Recent innovations, such as real-time voice recognition language translation or controlling the playback of video by just looking at your device (both innovations used in new Samsung devices) will seem like common technology in the near future.

This means that the increase in capabilities of the devices we use will enable us to do new things that we won't be currently thinking about. It is also likely that the role a mobile device currently takes in bridging the gap between the physical world and the online world will continue and grow.

The near future

Google's 'Glass' product (see Figure 7.1) is a glimpse of a very near future that combines a wearable mobile device that provides augmented reality, voice recognition and a range of functionality via internet connection. The product is already in existence and Google, as well as external developers, are building and refining what it will be able to do.

FIGURE 7.1   Google Glass: augmented reality wearable technology (www.google.com/glass)

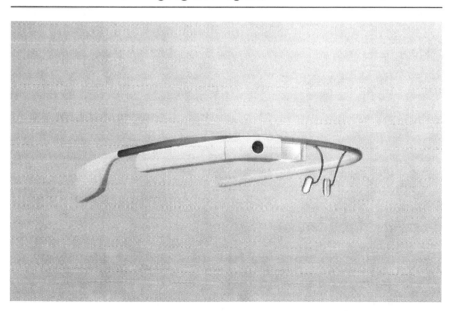

Although Google Glass takes fairly widely available technologies, combines them and then wraps them in some clever software, it is causing a major reaction. This is in part due to the clever use of technology, but more about the idea of wearing technology and the idea of being 'constantly connected'. (You can clearly just take the glasses off or switch them off at any point. I'm also pretty sure they don't have an everlasting battery yet either.)

Whenever I show Google Glass to a room full of students, delegates on a training course or an audience at a larger presentation, the audience seems to be divided between two points of view. One group of people is excited by the possibilities and impressed by the technology. The other group finds the prospect and implications of being connected so much more directly to the internet disturbing or distressing.

Mobile changing society

This reaction is interesting for many reasons, but most of all it shows how mobile technology is changing our day-by-day lives so fundamentally. Essentially, the technology is moving more quickly than society is adapting to it and developing cultural norms in how to deal with it.

I see a great example of this every time I talk at a conference. A few years ago, if I was speaking on stage and somebody was looking down at their phone, it was a sign that I didn't have their attention. This may have been due to my talk being boring, them having more important things to deal with, or the fact that they weren't really interested in the first place. Now when I speak at a conference most people are looking down at their phones. It may be that I am getting increasingly boring, but based on the level of tweets and social media posts, what they are actually doing is broadcasting snippets from my talk in real time.

Double-edged sword

This change in behaviour has both good and bad sides. Firstly, it's great because it means the members of the audience think there is value in what I am saying, enough value in fact to share it with their own, wider audience. That means in turn that I have a wider audience and will gain a larger social media following myself.

The downside is that it means the audience isn't fully listening to what I'm saying and their engagement with my content may be fairly superficial: looking for sound-bites of content to publish.

This double-edged sword is a reflection of two issues in my opinion. Firstly, we haven't developed a culture around these kinds of circumstances yet to have worked out what is the best pattern of behaviour. Secondly, the technology is still getting in the way.

The ideal solution is not only a cultural one, where known behaviour is expected (for example, you turn your mobile off or to silent in the cinema), but also one of better technology. Technology that didn't require me to look down at my mobile device and use my hands to interact with it would mean that posting social media updates would be far less interruptive.

Frictionless technology

Reducing how much the technology gets in the way of what I am trying to do and creating a more seamless experience is what 'frictionless' technology is all about. We could compare what technology we need to carry now to create, edit and publish a video. Twenty years ago it would have meant a lot of heavy and very expensive equipment. Now it means carrying the average smartphone.

The reaction Google Glass has created because of its wearable nature and the fact that it overlays something onto our 'real world' will become more and more relevant in the very near future. As mobile technology develops, the device itself becomes less and less relevant, and the utility it offers has the opportunity to be more and more frictionless.

Some fairly obvious examples come to mind very easily if you just look at Google Glass. How about taking the experience of watching somebody on stage giving a presentation and trying to make the follow-up actions simpler? Using facial recognition you could automatically be shown the speakers' online profiles, previous work and other similar experts. Another example scenario could be that you have gone for a walk in the woods and see a snake. Google Glass could identify the snake, take a picture and post it to your social networks to share your experience, and most importantly, tell you if it's dangerous or not.

The point is that it's so easy to think of a thousand day-to-day experiences that could be enhanced in some way by using these kinds of technologies. And all of these changes in our everyday experiences will mean that mobile technology becomes more and more personal. You only have to have lost your phone once to realize that we are increasingly reliant and connected to the devices we use.

Privacy and the future of mobile

The overlap between mobile marketing, search and social media is creating circumstances where questions of privacy are increasingly being discussed and challenged.

One of the key features demonstrated in an early Google Glass promotion video (which actually showed a mock-up of its expected functionality rather what it could actually do at that time) was the wearer of the device asking where his friend was, and his friend's location being immediately shown on the augmented reality display. This particular piece of functionality was always the one that seemed to draw the biggest gasps from an audience because of the implications this could have on privacy. The reality is that smartphone-based geographic location data has been around for some time, but its usage is one of the many things about sharing so much data that is increasingly concerning people.

The key issue at play is that of value exchange and transparency. If I share data with you, am I fully aware of that fact and do I know what you will do with that data? The other question, which consumers are increasingly asking, is: what do you offer me in exchange?

A clear value exchange proposition is going to become increasingly important when we attempt any form of mobile marketing. If I give you my data, what functionality, or other value, will you give me in exchange? Then finally, and most importantly, do I trust you enough to give you my data?

The distant future

Really this section should be entitled 'The seems distant, but will actually probably be a lot sooner than we think, future'. It's not all that catchy though, so we'll stick with 'distant future'. If we go back to the exponential growth analogy of filling a stadium with water, we can see that the rate of change got pretty radical pretty quickly.

This could mean some very significant changes to the world around us. A very clear point, in my opinion, is the idea that 'mobile technology' will become irrelevant (and some would argue it already is). The integration of technology into everything we do, and even into us as human beings, will mean that the funny little devices we carry around now will in the future seem like the Dark Ages do to us now.

Consider that it's a fairly logical train of thought, that we will all be constantly connected to the internet (whatever that looks like then!), wherever we go. It's also not unreasonable to think that computing power and artificial intelligence will have radically advanced and machines will be far more 'intelligent'. (When you start to consider that sentient life may not be limited to organic organisms, we start to get a little too science fiction for the remit of this book I'm afraid). It's also a fairly logical path that would lead us to think we can control and interact with devices by thinking, since you can already get games that allow you to use your brain waves to control physical objects (MindWave from NeuroSky).

These relatively logical progressions of technology mean that the world we live in will be radically changed. I find this extremely exciting and feel very blessed to live in such fast changing times. If, however, this all fills you with a sense of dread, bear in mind it's the application not the technology that's the issue. When video cassettes first came into usage by the general population, there were huge concerns about 'video nasties'. We adjusted and the world continued.

A guaranteed future prediction

The only guarantee is that the pace of change within the arena of digital technology, and the rate at which this impacts our organizations and wider society, will get faster and faster. Organizations (and individuals) that are able to adapt to ongoing change will be best placed to survive and thrive in this environment.

Let's get practical

And now we move from the future of artificial intelligence and controlling technology with your mind, to the slightly more practical aspects of mobile marketing. Part Two of this book is your hands-on guide to implementing mobile marketing in the real world.

PART TWO
The tactical
toolkit

Introduction

Part Two of the book is a practical guide to each of the key technologies and practical challenges involved with mobile marketing. It has been written so that you can either read it progressively (just like a normal book), but also as a reference that can be dipped in and out of in the order that is most appropriate to your current challenges.

However, I would advise you to try and learn about all of the aspects of mobile marketing, even if the particular topic or technology doesn't seem relevant for your current situation. Increasingly, the practicalities of technologies involved have an impact on one another and should make up part of an integrated campaign.

Also look out for the highlighted boxes of content. These contain additional information, examples and practical tips that can help save you time and stress when implementing your digital campaigns.

> ### Latest techniques and best practice
>
> Don't forget that you can find examples of the latest mobile marketing techniques, tools and best practice on our website. You can also ask me questions directly and share your experiences:
> **http://www.targetinternet.com/mobilemarketing/**.

09 Mobile sites and responsive design

Let's make something clear from the outset; you need a mobile-optimized site. That doesn't mean your site happens to work on mobile devices. It means the user journey via mobile has been carefully considered and you offer the optimal experience via mobile devices. It means that you have weighed up the different technical solutions in order to achieve this and have selected the most appropriate approach. It also means that you have not been steered by the limitations of your current web platform or content management system (CMS).

In this chapter we'll explore why a mobile site really is absolutely essential, why apps and mobile sites aren't a one-or-the-other choice, and how you can achieve your marketing and business objectives using mobile sites.

Start with the fundamentals

Already, an average of 23 per cent of visitors to many sites get there via mobile devices (Walker Sands, 2013). This means that, potentially, nearly a quarter of your audience will be on a mobile device. This is reason enough to make sure your site is fully optimized for these visitors, before you even consider the potential of increased conversion rates and average order values via a properly optimized mobile experience. Increased average order values of up to 22 per cent have been demonstrated through properly optimized mobile experience (Affiliate Window, 2013).

Focus on the user journey

The key point of a mobile-optimized site is to offer an experience that best suits the consumers' needs and circumstances. This means they should be able to access the information or utility that your site offers, on the device they are using, in an easy and efficient way.

Classic mistakes

Mobile compatible

Having a website that works on mobile devices often confuses people into thinking they have a mobile-optimized experience. If your website works on mobile devices, but the consumer spends much of his or her time zooming in and out to see anything clearly, this is not an optimized experience.

Broken journey

Adopting the latest technology trends without considering the impact they have on the user journey is a common mistake. Placing a QR code onto your latest outdoor advertising campaign, without considering the fact that the website you are sending mobile users through to does not work on mobile devices, is not a great idea.

Mobile site dead end

This is my pet hate. It involves visiting a website on a mobile device and then being re-directed to a mobile-specific version of the website. Nothing disastrous so far, but there is nothing more annoying than finding the piece of content I need isn't on their mobile site, but their technology won't let me visit their standard site on my mobile device. Every time I try and visit the main site it just re-directs me. Give people an option to visit the standard website. Please.

Mobile site options

One size fits all

The first, simplest and least likely to work approach! The idea is that you create one site that works well on desktop and mobile devices. In reality, it normally means that some sacrifices have to be made and that either your desktop or mobile site will need to suffer.

The only scenario in which this really works is when your site is very simple and limited in its functionality. An example of this would be a site based on a single landing page with a sign-up form.

What we are really doing in this scenario quite often is tweaking a website so it at least functions correctly on a mobile device. This clearly isn't a mobile-optimized site, but it may be what you need to do as an interim measure.

What this highlights is that we need to start by understanding what should be the key differences between a mobile and desktop experience and why? We'll explore this in the next section of this chapter.

Dedicated mobile site

A mobile-specific version of your website can seem like the most obvious solution. Basically, you have two versions of your website, a mobile and desktop version, and depending on the device the site visitor is using, they are given a different version of your site.

You could in fact have multiple versions beyond a desktop and mobile version, and have versions for individual devices or maybe just separate desktop, smartphone and tablet versions.

The advantage of this approach is the ability to completely adjust a site for an optimized mobile experience. The downside is that you have multiple sites to manage and this can create a few challenges.

The level of complexity this creates will depend on how you update and manage the content of your sites. Static sites, which are sites that are updated and edited by changing the code itself (using a developer or updating it yourself), just mean increased workloads as you have multiple sites to update. Content-managed sites, which are sites where you have some form of interface that allows you to update your site, can be more complex.

CMS can be used in a number of different ways to manage mobile sites:

- **A CMS-based desktop site and static mobile site** – this means you have a mobile-optimized site built but in order to edit and change it, you will need to use a developer or edit the code directly yourself.

- **A CMS-based desktop site and separate CMS for your mobile site** – this means you will have two separate CMSs in order to update the different versions of your sites. This makes the movement of content between the two sites more complex, but can be a fairly straightforward solution.

- **A single CMS for multiple versions of your site** – this means that although you have a separate mobile-optimized site, you are able to manage your site content for multiple sites under one CMS. Generally this solution will allow you to edit content and 'assign' it to a particular version of your site. This is a fairly elegant solution but requires a CMS that is designed to manage this kind of situation.

Responsive design

Responsive design, sometimes referred to as adaptive design (although these definitions actually mean different things that we'll discuss later), means developing one site that will display appropriately for each device it is viewed on. This means the site can look completely different on each device and will lay out in the way best suited to a particular environment.

This approach is generally implemented using a combination of web technologies like cascading style sheets (CSS) and Javascript which we'll discuss more in a moment. The key point is that these technologies allow the browser to look at things such as the device the site visitor is using, the width and height of the display, and then decide on how the page should be laid out. Figure 9.1 shows the CSS-Tricks website, a great example of responsive design in practice. On the left is the full width version, on the right the same site with the browser width reduced (**http://www.css-tricks.com**).

FIGURE 9.1 The CSS-Tricks website (www.css-tricks.com)

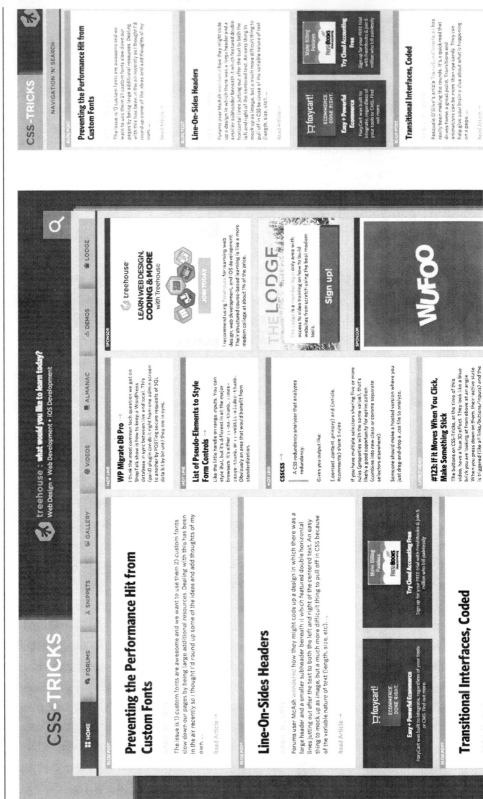

Responsive vs adaptive design

Responsive design and adaptive design are often terms that are used interchangeably; however, they are quite distinct things.

Responsive design is something that is actioned within your browser. This means that a page is sent to your browser, and your browser then does the work to display the correct elements of the page. This is called a client-side technology (the client is your browser).

Adaptive design is something that is actioned on the web server. The type of device being used is identified and then the appropriate version of the site is delivered. This is called a server-side technology.

The advantage of adaptive design is that not as much content is sent to the browser where it may not be used and a solely mobile version of a site is sent to a mobile device. (See the next box on responsive design and its limitations).

The term responsive design is gradually coming to mean adaptive design, although developers will argue about the differences for ever more.

Hybrid approach

There are also some solutions that take elements of dedicated mobile sites and combine them with some responsive design elements. For example, your site could use a number of CSSs to make your site look different on different devices, but your CMS could allow you to select which pages, menu options and other features display on different versions of your site. This essentially amounts to a dedicated mobile site but can help minimize the management time involved in having multiple sites.

There are also other technologies that can be combined with responsive design to get past its limitations and to create an optimized mobile experience. These are often referred to as 'responsive web design with server-side components' or RESS for short.

A silver bullet for mobile sites

Responsive design is often seen as a silver bullet solution, solving all of our mobile site problems. It certainly can offer a single site solution, meaning that your website adapts according to the device of the visitor. There are, however, some considerations you need to be aware of.

Firstly, you need to consider if a responsively designed site can go far enough to really implement a mobile-optimized experience, or whether you are still making compromises because of the limitations of the technology? It's certainly possible to achieve an optimized experience in most scenarios, but this very much depends on how your site is implemented and what functionality you require. In many cases, for example, e-commerce sites still need a dedicated mobile site as responsive design just doesn't give enough flexibility to adapt the site as much as is required.

Another consideration should be load time. If responsive design is implemented poorly, you can end up loading a full desktop site to a mobile device, and then just displaying certain elements of it. For this reason, it is generally a better bet to start considering responsive design from the outset of a web project rather than trying to bolt it on afterwards, as this often leads to 'bloated' websites that can be slow to load.

Rather than being a silver bullet, responsive design techniques are just that: techniques. They can certainly help you achieve a mobile-optimized experience, but you should also be aware of their limitations and they can be used in combination with other techniques.

Mobile design principles: mobile sites vs desktop sites

So let's take a look in the following section at the key considerations when we are considering mobile sites and the main differences from a desktop version of a website.

Prioritization of content

One of the key issues with mobile devices is generally their screen size and the fact that screens are smaller than those of a desktop or laptop computer. This means that page 'real estate' is at a premium and we need to make viewing and understanding the content as easy as possible.

This generally means considering the user journey of a mobile user and prioritizing content according to their potential needs. It also means filtering out content that may not be essential in order to de-clutter the mobile experience.

Horizontal vs vertical layout

Smartphones are generally used initially in vertical layout as are tablet devices. Screens on desktop devices, however, are generally horizontally orientated. This orientation needs to be factored into our designs, but we also need to consider the fact that mobile devices can change orientation.

Links and buttons

Throughout websites we use hyperlinks extensively, and hyperlinks are just linked text. This approach is less effective on mobile devices because of the size of screens relative to our input device, ie our fingers. For this reason, buttons tend to work better on mobile devices but can look extremely clunky on desktop sites.

Screen size and graphics

Quite clearly we are generally dealing with smaller screen sizes and we have already discussed how screen space is at a premium. However, this lack of space and screen size means that many graphics that are suitable for desktop-based sites are not suitable on mobile sites. This is generally due to the lack of clarity when an image is small and because of the amount of space they are taking up in the precious amount of space available.

Reduced hierarchy

Many desktop-based sites offer various ways of navigating their content, hierarchical menu systems and page elements like breadcrumb trails that show where you are on the site. Because of space limitations we often need to remove many of these elements. However, it is also essential that the mobile user does not feel lost or confused as to where they are on the site. For this reason, having a reduced and simpler hierarchy on your mobile site can make things much easier.

Phone integration

Phones clearly have additional functionality not offered by desktop devices that can often be used within mobile sites (apps can generally access these functionalities even more effectively and we'll discuss that in the apps chapter later). Things like geographic location, click to maps, click to text and so on can be utilized to improve the mobile experience.

Technology and jargon in perspective

When talking about mobile site development, there are a lot of technical terms and technologies involved. Below you'll find a few of the most important ones that should help you navigate, discuss and develop your mobile site plans:

- **HTML** – hypertext markup language (HTML) is the markup language that is used to lay out web pages. The files sent to our web browsers when we request a web page are HTML files which are then translated by the browser into what we see.

- **CSS** – cascading style sheets (CSS) is used to describe the styling information for a markup language. This basically means it defines what different parts of a web page should look like. A range of CSS can be used on different devices to generate varying content layout.

- **Javascript** – Javascript is a client-side language (meaning it is run and used within a browser) to add extra functionality to web pages. It is often used to help select which is the most appropriate CSS to use on a particular device.

- **Responsive design** – responsive design allows web pages to be displayed differently on different devices by adjusting the layout and page elements shown. These adjustments are made within the browser.

- **Adaptive design** – adaptive design allows for a specific version of a web page to be sent to a specific device or browser. Once the device and/or browser is known, only the relevant version of the web page is sent to the browser.

- **Progressive enhancement** – this is an approach to building web pages that tries to prevent sending content to basic browsers that wouldn't be compatible with it. This means a basic version of a web page is built and then gradually enhanced for more sophisticated browsers. The more sophisticated elements of the page are not loaded initially, meaning there is no wasted load time.

- **RESS** – responsive web design with server-side components (RESS) is a technique combining elements of responsive web design and other technologies to maximize the mobile experience and bypass shortcomings of individual techniques. RESS is also often referred to as adaptive design.

- **Media queries** – these are part of CSS and an important part of responsive design. They allow the layout to adapt to the screen resolution and layout.

- **Fluid grid** – the fluid grid principle is that web pages should be positioned and laid out according to percentages rather than fixed sizes and positions. This means that layouts can more easily be adapted for different sizes of screens.

Mobile site and responsive design examples

For some great examples of mobile sites and to see responsive design in practice, visit our website: **http://www.targetinternet.com/mobilemarketing**.

What responsive design really means

When many people talk about responsive design, they are in fact talking about using a number of different technologies to achieve an optimal mobile experience. These differing ways of using the same phrase is why you'll find so much discussion online about the pros and cons of responsive design.

In reality, when most people talk about responsive design they are actually talking about a number of techniques working together and are actually referring to RESS techniques or other hybrid solutions.

The 3-step quick and dirty guide to a responsive website

I wish somebody had given me the following advice at the beginning of my digital marketing career as it would have saved me lots and lots of pain in building websites from scratch, on bespoke CMS, and wrangling over expensive functionality improvements to my sites.

This is not supposed to be a thorough website specification building process, and in fact it ignores nearly all of the key steps I would normally go through in order to get a professional website built. It ignores usability principles, mapping the user journey, content auditing and a million other key and valid principles. What it does do though is demonstrate how quickly you actually get a responsive site up and running. Whether that site will deliver on your marketing objectives is a different question!

All behold the mighty Wordpress!

Let us be absolutely clear that I love Wordpress. I think it is one of the best things that has ever happened to the web and I am unapologetically enthusiastic about it! The simple reason is that it makes building many types of websites quick, easy and cost effective. This includes mobile websites and using responsive design.

FIGURE 9.2   Wordpress software from Wordpress.org (www.wordpress.org)

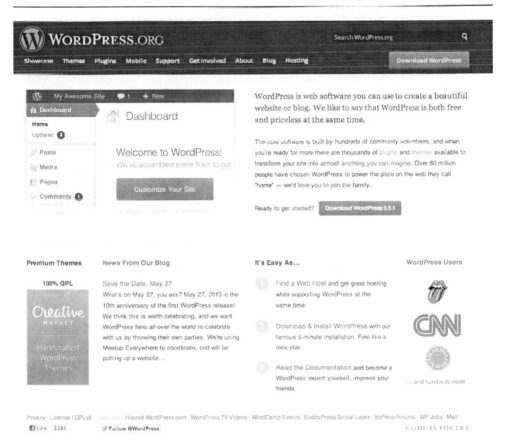

Wordpress started out as an open source (meaning it is free to use) blogging platform. It is still a blogging platform, but in reality it is a highly flexible content management system capable of building and managing websites of most types – and it's free.

If you go to Wordpress.com you can set up a Wordpress blog and have it up and running in minutes. This blog will be hosted by Wordpress and you will have a vast, but slightly limited, set of capabilities to build websites.

The alternative approach, and one that we are discussing here, is to go to Wordpress.org (see Figure 9.2) where the software can be downloaded and installed onto your own servers and customized as much as needed. You can do this yourself if you have the technical skills (see the box below on the kind of skills you'll need and that are worth having).

Step 1: Get some hosting

You're going to need some hosting space online that is capable of hosting Wordpress. This hosting will generally require two things: the ability to process PHP, the language in which Wordpress is written; and the ability to have a database, so you'll need MySQL on the server as well.

Before you run away in panic, as this is all starting to sound quite technical, lots of hosting companies have packages designed specifically for Wordpress hosting and many come with it pre-installed. Wordpress even give you a guide to hosting and recommend some companies (see **http://wordpress.org/hosting/**).

Step 2: Select a responsive theme

Wordpress uses something called 'themes' to customize the look and feel of your site. This is where the responsive design part comes in. You can buy Wordpress themes on hundreds of websites (and actually download many for free as well), and these themes are uploaded into your implementation of Wordpress. Once uploaded you can choose to preview what your site will look like with the theme, and choose to then 'switch it on'. Most themes come with a number of customization options, including things like changing colours, menu options and types of page layouts. This means that when you preview the site, you won't normally see what it will finally look like, but it will give you some insights.

You need to make sure that you select a theme that is designed to be responsive and work on mobile devices. These responsive themes come with a number of mobile customization options, like allowing you to select what menu options will show on a mobile version of the site and what content should be visible. As such, these sites offer a good combination of true, responsive design and elements of building a mobile-specific version of your site, all working within one CMS.

There are lots of Wordpress theme websites out there, and a Google search of the phrase 'Wordpress theme' will give you a huge amount to look through and get a feel for the kind of things that are available. You can normally preview what your website could potentially look like and the theme websites also explain the customization options that will be available to you.

My favourite theme website is **http://www.themeforest.net** and it's actually where the theme for the website that accompanies this book was bought!

We've also listed some more of our favourite Wordpress theme websites on our website at **http://www.targetiternet.com/mobilemarketing/**.

Figure 9.3 shows a wedding photography website built in Wordpress using a downloadable responsive theme. Figure 9.4 illustrates the same website as seen on an iPhone, showing the mobile, one column design, with menu navigation shown as a drop down menu that launches a mobile selector. We'll discuss mobile design later in this chapter.

Step 3.1: Define your customization and get a freelancer to implement

At this stage you have two choices. Do you want to try and install Wordpress, install your theme and then customize things, or do you want somebody to do all of this for you? If you don't really need any major customization and you think you can manage the skills in the box below, it's a great learning curve to do this yourself. If you need a fair bit of customization, don't want to bother with this type of thing or are nervous about your technical abilities, there is a quick and cost effective alternative.

There are a number of websites that allow you to submit a brief for a project and allow freelancers or companies around the world to give you a quote and submit their services for the work. My favourite of these websites is **http://www.elance.com** and it is where I have found the developers that I work with on a regular basis now.

The most important thing about using one of these freelance websites is to make sure you submit a thorough and well-thought-out

FIGURE 9.3 Website built in Wordpress using downloadable responsive theme (www.simplyweddingphotography.co.uk)

Simply Wedding Photography
Affordable Wedding and Civil Partnership Photograpy

Home   Image Gallery   Weddings   Civil Partnerships   Prices   About me

Affordable Photography

Simply Wedding Photography offers affordable wedding and civil partnership photography that does not compromise on quality or style for couples getting married in Sussex.

My aim is to offer people the wedding photographs that they want at a price that they can afford.

Based in Brighton, I will travel to West Sussex and East Sussex and will consider other locations on request.

Prices overview

All the packages include a minimum of 150 High resolution photographs of your Wedding Day on a CD ROM - If more photographs are taken on the day you will also receive these.

Wedding Photos Price Package 1 £450.00
Ceremony and Reception (3hrs)

Wedding Photos Price Package 2 £600.00
Getting ready, Ceremony and Reception (5hrs)

Wedding Photos Price Package 3 £800.00
Getting ready, Ceremony, Reception and Meal (7hrs)

Testimonials

"Susana offers an excellent service which is outstanding value for money. She really did capture our wedding day just as we remember it."

"I wanted my day to be a relaxed as possible and Susana reflected this perfectly in her photographs."

"Thank you for the photo's. We love all of them and are busy showing them to everyone"

FIGURE 9.4   Same website on an iPhone
(www.simplyweddingphotography.co.uk)

'brief', or in other words, a project specification. The more detailed, clear and unambiguous your specification, the more likely that the work delivered by the freelancer will be what you were hoping for and expecting. This specification may include things like text describing functionality of your mobile site; screen shots indicating where you'd like changes; scanned sketches or diagrams communicating your ideas clearly.

Once you submit your specification you then sit back and wait for developers to submit their quotes. When the quotes do start to come in, your next big problem is selecting which one to choose. Cost will obviously be a factor, but more importantly you need to judge the freelancers' abilities and understanding of your project specification. You'll also need to consider things like reliability, project management skills and communication skills. Bear in mind your freelancer might be on the other side of the planet, and that you may not share the same first language. I am based in the UK and work regularly with developers in Turkey and India via Elance.com with absolutely no problems.

A good way to select a freelancer is to look at their response and see if they seem to understand your specification clearly. You then normally look at their work experience and see how much work they have completed on the freelancer site you are using. You can normally see how many jobs they have completed, their overall total billings (so you can get a feel for the scale of projects they are working on) and what their feedback is like on previous projects.

Just like any online review, we need to know how to differentiate good, useful and honest reviews from those that have been placed falsely in order to try and persuade you into placing work with a particular freelancer. My experience has shown that the amount of fake reviews on sites like these is fairly low, but there are some signs to look out for. The most obviously suspicious sign is when there only a few reviews, all on very low-cost projects, that all appear to be in the same tone and use similar language. This can show that the freelancer in question has posted jobs, completed them him- or herself and then left their own reviews!

A great way to minimize the risk is to post a small, low-cost job first of all and try out a freelancer. If you find they are reliable and effective you may then want to scale up to do more work with them. My experience using freelancers this way has been absolutely exceptional, and I am still amazed at what great work I can get done at such low cost. Although I can do lots of customization work myself, it is often easier and faster to get it done by a freelancer.

Step 3.2: Install Wordpress and your theme

If you are feeling confident of your skills or you are keen to learn, setting up your own Wordpress site and installing the theme yourself can be very straightforward. However, if you want to do customization beyond the basic functionality of Wordpress (changing text and images, for example) and beyond what your theme offers as standard, you will need more in-depth technical skills.

Wordpress actually offers a very clear step by step guide to installing the system and there are very active discussion forums where you scan previous issues and ask questions. Get started by reading this installation guide: **http://codex.wordpress.org/Installing_WordPress.**

Useful hands-on skills

If you want to be able to deploy a Wordpress website yourself, you're going to need the following very simple skills. If you have no interest whatsoever in doing something like this yourself, it's still worth understanding some of the key steps involved.

Hosting control panels

Most hosting, and particularly hosting of the kind you'll need for Wordpress, will generally come with a control panel. There are normally two levels of control panels: one for managing your hosting account and one for actually managing your web server. We are most interested in the web server control panel. This will allow you to do things like set up e-mail addresses and a database. There are common platforms for doing these kinds of things, and cPanel and Plesk are two of the most popular. They are generally very easy to use and fairly intuitive. Normally the most complicated thing you'll need to do is to create a database, which basically involves clicking on a 'database' icon, selecting something like 'create' and then giving it a name and password. Most often, the database element of your web hosting will use something called MySQL, and your web control panel is allowing you to interact with this in an easy way.

FTP software

In order to put files onto your web hosting space, you are going to need some file transfer protocol (FTP) software. There are plenty of different solutions out there for PC, Mac and even for mobile devices. Your hosting will come with an FTP username and password, and you'll need to put these into your software in order to navigate your web server and add/remove files.

HTML and PHP

You really don't need to know any PHP (a server-side scripting language) or HTML to install Wordpress. However, I think it's increasingly important that more of us understood some of the technologies behind how the web works. I'm not suggesting that we should all go out and become developers, but a good knowledge of how the different technologies work and fit together can be massively useful. It will allow you to interact with developers more easily, mean you can understand what you are being told, and know how to ask the right kinds of questions. It also means you'll be much better at writing project specifications. A great place to learn the fundamentals (and beyond) are the tutorials on WebMonkey that can be found at: **http://www.webmonkey.com/tutorials/**.

That's pretty much it. Combine these skills (and you can skip the HTML and PHP bit) with a download of Wordpress and some hosting, and you'll be able to set up your own website. There are also some more great tutorials online and we've listed some of these on our website: **http://www.targetinternet.com/mobilemarketing/**.

A user-centred approach to mobile sites

Just like all web design, all mobile site design and planning should start by considering some key questions. What are our business objectives and how does our mobile approach tie in with this? What are the users' requirements and how can we help them achieve these requirements using a mobile site? Once we are sure that these two questions are answered and aligned we can then start to build our mobile site.

However, we always need to remember much of the design process is based on theory, planning and assumptions (no matter how well researched this work is). Therefore we need to make sure we factor in user testing and ongoing improvement into our mobile site development process. Let's work through some of the key stages, as illustrated in Figure 9.5.

FIGURE 9.5   Mobile design and development: key elements of user-centred approach

Current situation and business objectives

Although it may seem strange to suggest the first step of a *user-centred* approach is to think about business objectives, we need to frame the entire process. We need to consider how a mobile site aligns with our over-arching business objectives and define the purpose for which it exists. It is very easy to create mobile sites, apps, use social media or carry out any digital activity for the sake of doing it, rather than actually having a clear alignment with business objectives.

It may be that a mobile site is essential to help potential customers research our products and services effectively. It may be that the functionality we offer gives the user something useful that helps bolster our value proposition in the market. Whatever the business objectives, this should frame our plans and can help inform budgetary decisions and help us get internal buy-in where needed.

We should also at this stage benchmark our current situation and the environment we are working in. Some of the questions you need to answer are suggested below·

- How does a mobile site align with my business objectives?
- How much of our existing traffic is on mobile devices?
- What is the current mobile experience?
- How do we currently rank in the search engines for mobile search?
- What do our competitors offer via mobile sites?
- How do our competitors rank in the search engines for mobile search?
- What resources do we have, what can we commit and what will be the ongoing requirements?
- What skills do we have in-house and what partnerships do we have to achieve this project?

Once we have benchmarked our current situation we can move on to trying to understand the potential mobile site user. Always remember though, this should be seen as an iterative process, and you may need to revisit this step a number of times as new questions and challenges arise.

User requirements

At this stage we get into the essential process of trying to understand the key user requirements. There is enough theory on this topic to fill the rest of the book very easily. Don't worry, we won't do that. We'll focus on the key issues, best practice, and point out some great resources on the topic.

User-centred design resources

As normal you can find more resources on our website: **http://www.targetinternet.com/mobilemarketing/**.

It's also worth checking out the site below as well. It's my favourite resource on all things about usability by the great company WebCredible (no commercial relationship!): **http://www.webcredible.co.uk/user-friendly-resources/**.

There are a number of theories on how best to understand user requirements, so I've highlighted some key options below. Essentially we are trying to understand the tasks mobile site users will be carrying out and what their end goals are. Once we understand this, we should be able to develop a mobile site that helps the user to carry out these tasks and achieve their goals in the most effective way possible.

Personas

Personas are fictional characters that try to encompass as many of the characteristics of the target audience as possible. Any set audience may encompass a number of different personas, and these personas can be created to varying levels of detail.

A basic persona may just include things like key needs, desires and motivators, whereas a very detailed persona may be given an elaborate background story including work details, family, personal values and demographics like age and location.

The aim of the persona is to give us something to test our mobile designs against and allows us to ask some key questions. Would the design we have suggested match the needs of this persona? How would the needs of different personas vary, and how does this impact our design?

The following is a very brief example persona. It describes an individual and highlights the key issues in their life that may impact what they want and need from any particular mobile site:

Example persona

Susana is a mid-thirties professional woman with two children and a very busy life. She is technically savvy and an early adopter of many technologies. She needs the technology she uses to be reliable and robust as it is used during work and family time. Her key motivators are lack of time, need to balance work and family life, as well a desire to be stylish and express her creative side.

So from this example we can start to make a number of assumptions about what will be important in our mobile site. The context of how this persona will impact our design will depend on our business objectives and the scenario we are working within.

Scenarios

Scenarios are imagined circumstances in which we place our personas, and map out the key circumstances, needs and activities that may occur. This means as well as using the persona to understand individual needs, the scenario gives us the context. This can include things like physical location at a particular time, a set of circumstances or events, as well as external factors such as time pressures.

Example scenario

Your persona is travelling to a business conference and needs to find out as much about your organization as possible while travelling and at the conference. The conference itself is only for a few hours and there is limited internet connectivity.

From this scenario we can see that ease of navigation (due to using a mobile device while travelling), prioritization of content (due to limited time) and a focus on fast downloads speeds (due to limited bandwidth), will all be important.

Use cases

A use case is a step-by-step description of the interaction between the persona and the mobile device/mobile site. This allows us to map how the device and mobile site will be interacted with, click by click. It also allows us to see the steps that are being taken by the persona and to understand how the flow of a particular task can be optimized.

Example use case

1 The user searches for the company name on their device in Google.

2 The Google search returns results with the company name.

3 The user clicks on the company search result.

4 The mobile version of the website is loaded.

5 The user then clicks on the menu to find the 'About Us' section of the site.

6 The About Us page loads.

7 The user scans the page to look for key information.

8 The user clicks on the 'Find Us at Conference X' logo.

9 A PDF document is downloaded showing stand location.

This use case serves a number of purposes. It gives us something with which to explore how the user will interact with the site and what the ideal steps are to achieve the user's objectives. It also allows us to consider the scenario in more detail and consider how this will impact the functionality and design that we must provide.

Once we have fully defined our user requirements we can then move into the next stage of implementation. Bear in mind though, that up until this stage, all of our planning, even if detailed and well thought out, is mostly based on assumptions.

Define, design, develop, validate, iterate

This stage of the process is all about testing our assumptions in the real world. We use the previous two stages (current situation and user requirements) to help us define what our mobile site should do, and how it should do it. We then look at the output from the user requirements stage in more detail and use this to design our mobile site.

The initial design should take the form of a prototype. A prototype is a version of the site that has not required full development but gives us enough to start testing our assumptions. We can then take this prototype and test it against the personas, scenarios and use cases we have developed. This will allow us to start to iterate our ideas and improve them according to all of the research and planning work we have already done.

We may also be able to use these prototypes (which may be just wireframe sketches of what the site will look like and how pages are connected to one another) and test them in the real world. An interview process with some members of our potential audience can help us test and improve our ideas further.

At this stage, when we are happy we have refined and revised our plans as much as possible, we then commit to the development of our mobile site. We hold back on this stage, until we are sure we have thoroughly tested our assumptions, because changing things after the development stage can become expensive, whereas changing at the prototyping stage is generally far lower cost.

Prototyping and wireframes

Wireframes are representations of what your site will be laid out like, showing the key elements of the page without any detailed design. These wireframes can be highly effective in mapping out ideas, before we get distracted by the graphical design elements of our sites. Clickable wireframes allow us to click through these wireframe diagrams and see how pages are connected to one another. This can allow for a basic form of user testing to see if navigation aligns with users' expectations.

My favourite wireframing tool is Balsamiq Mockups (see Figure 9.6). It's easy to use and allows you to create clickable wireframes very quickly: http://www.balsamiq.com/products/mockups.

Only once we are happy with the layout and functionality, and we have tested our designs against our assumptions, should we start thinking about graphic design. When I say graphic design, I am referring to the visual identity graphical elements of our mobile sites. I say this because if we go out and ask a designer to mock up our site early on in the development process, it is very likely that we are going to get

FIGURE 9.6   Example wireframe in Balsamiq Mockups

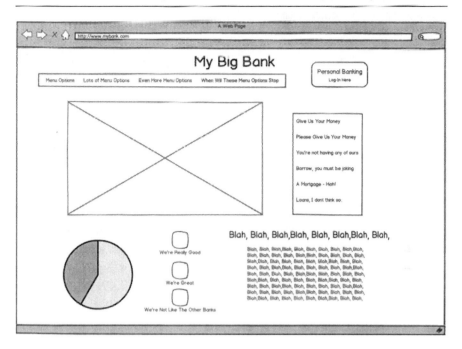

distracted by these designs. The reality is that a user-centred approach should consider functionality first; then graphic design when applied to this can enhance and improve it. However, the most beautiful site in the world will be useless if you don't get the functionality right.

I am certainly not dismissing graphic design as unimportant. I actually believe that the visual elements of a site can enhance the functionality massively when thought out correctly. We just shouldn't decide what something should look like, before we know what it does.

The final stage after prototyping is development, when we actually start to build our sites. No site is ever completed, mobile or otherwise. The first iteration of your site should be just that, an iteration. Even when you get to what you believe is the final version of your site, soon enough the environment in which you are operating will change and you will need to start testing, changing and improving again. From a budgetary perspective I never look at web development as a one-off cost. It should be something that is budgeted for as an ongoing cost and a project that is always developing.

Testing on mobile devices

There is no true alternative for actually testing on each of the mobile devices you are expecting your audience to use. However, there are a number of great online services that can help you test your mobile sites out if you don't have access to the particular device you need.

A good place to start is to look at your existing web analytics (assuming you have some) and looking at what mobile devices your existing site is being accessed on. This will give you an initial hit list of what devices you need to test first.

Google's GoMoMeter gives you an indication of what your site is going to look like. It's limited to simulating a single mobile device, based on an Android phone, but it is extremely easy to use: **http://letsgomo.com/**.

The Mobile Phone Emulator site offers a whole range of different devices that you can simulate, allowing you to see what your site will look like on various platforms. It also has settings so that it can display these in real-life size on your computer screen: **http://www.mobilephoneemulator.com/**.

The sooner you can get real users trying out your site the better (in controlled circumstances!). What I mean is that when you have a version of your site that is useable, even if it is unfinished and still has bugs, invite some users to try it out. Since there may be lots of problems still with the site, you may wish to do this on a one-to-one basis. My general experience is that even fairly basic usability testing, like asking a number of people to carry out the same task, will highlight key issues with your designs.

So you work towards a 'final' design, test, learn and improve on an ongoing basis. At some point you must decide to go 'live' and release your new mobile site into the world. Make sure that there are easy ways for users to feed back to you, so you can continue to improve things.

Ongoing maintenance

Once you achieve your beautifully planned and designed mobile site, you need to remember that you must commit to ongoing maintenance. With the world of mobile marketing moving so quickly, new devices, operating systems and changing user requirements are going to mean your site needs to change. If you don't adjust, what was a perfect site will in a short period of time become a business problem.

Mobile sites: conclusions

As you can see, there is a lot to consider when building mobile sites. You need to understand the technical aspects of mobile sites, but most importantly you must think about the reasoning behind the site in the first place. Poor use of technology can ruin an otherwise well-thought-out mobile site, but a site without a user-centred design approach is unlikely to stand a chance in the first place.

10 How to build an app

At the time of writing, the Apple App Store has just passed 50 billion downloads and Apple is paying more than one billion US dollars per month to app developers (*Forbes*, 2013). This app 'gold rush' as it has been described, has led to a flurry of activity in the world of app development and the production of millions of apps. We'll look at the practicalities of building an app in this chapter, but first we are going to answer some essential questions and take a look at the app environment.

Many organizations rushed out and built apps just because they could. I witnessed dozens of conversations that started with the words 'We need an app' and ended in protracted discussion about what it could do, and how much it would cost. Just as we've discussed in the social media section of this book though: just because you can do something doesn't mean that you should.

Mobile sites first

If you don't have a mobile-optimized website, forget about getting an app built and get your site fixed first. We've already talked about the huge increase in traffic to sites on mobile devices, and the reality is that this is actually more likely to be a user's initial experience of your mobile presence than an app. It's not that apps aren't also important, and in fact some studies have found that 85 per cent of users prefer the experience of apps over mobile sites (Compuware, 2013), but in reality if you actually need an app, you most likely also need a mobile-optimized site.

Bolstering value proposition

Just like any marketing activity we need to start by aligning our business objectives with user requirements and decide how our app can help achieve this. One thing for which apps can be fantastic is bolstering value proposition by delivering some form of online utility or entertainment.

Nike Training Club bolsters value proposition

One of my favourite examples of using an app to bolster value proposition is the Nike Training Club (NTC) app (see Figure 10.1). It's very much in line with a clear value proposition of helping you achieve your athletic goals (rather than just being a company that makes sports clothes) and offers a range of features that are both practical, nicely designed and well thought out. The app is centrally focussed around positioning Nike as experts that help assist an individual with their particular fitness needs.

Beyond this core functionality, NTC does a few things that show how appropriate use of the technology can be highly effective in tying together business objectives and user requirements. The rewards programme adds a level of gamification that encourages users to achieve training goals and then share these achievements. Users are rewarded for this activity and this drives social sharing and builds visibility of the brand. However, most important in my view is the data collection opportunity this gives Nike. By understanding their target audience's training objectives, challenges and the practicalities of how they implement these plans, Nike gains valuable insights.

The production and distribution of the app are a sizeable investment, but when you compare this to the cost of running TV campaigns to build affinity and awareness, apps like this start to make a lot of financial success for a large brand like Nike. Also, bear in mind that the ongoing use of an app offers repeat brand exposure and can build affinity if the user requirements are met effectively.

FIGURE 10.1 Nike Training Club helps bolster value proposition (www.nike.com/us/en_gb/womens-training/apps/nike-training-club)

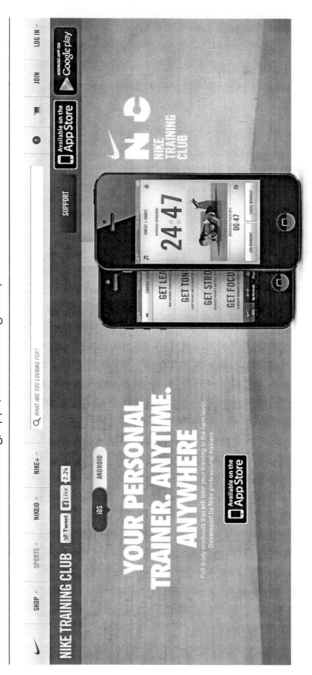

Before we look at the specifics of developing apps, and address things like 'native' apps vs 'web' apps, let's consider the entire process and cover the common steps that you'll go through whenever you are developing an app.

The app-building process

We've repeated this mantra time and time again in this book, but let's start with some clear objectives. Why are you actually building an app in the first place? Is it all about bolstering your value proposition as we've already discussed? Perhaps you are looking to build extra income so you can leave your job and live a life of travel and break the 9 to 5 routine (it's possible, but rare!). Maybe you want to use an app to help sell your product, or maybe you're just doing it to see if you can. Whatever the answer, you need to have very clear expectations about what help you are going to need and what you can expect in terms of costs and revenues.

Understanding the skills involved

You may have a fantastic idea for an app that you are convinced will help you achieve your objectives, but we need to start laying down the path that will lead that app into the real world. I've listed some of the core stages below that you'll need to consider:

- app idea and initial concepts;
- app specification and wireframing;
- user interface design;
- visual design;
- technical development;
- testing;
- app store submission;
- app marketing;
- app maintenance;
- customer support.

Hopefully you can see from this list that there is a lot more to the process than just coming up with an idea. In fact many excellent apps fail because of a lack of ongoing marketing plans or because of poor maintenance and customer support.

Because of this list of different skills involved, it generally means that you are going to need some support with creating your app from multiple sources. We'll take a look at each of these steps and examine some of the things you'll need to consider.

Specification and wireframing

Just as with the construction of mobile sites, it is almost certainly worth spending as much time as possible on this initial stage. If you get this part right, you'll save yourself a lot of time and pain later on. A highly detailed and clear specification will lay out exactly what you are trying to achieve and how it should work. It will also consider fundamental elements of the interface design, like highlighting how pages are connected to one another, the flow through the app and so on. This basic graphical process is known as 'wireframing' and it helps to communicate your expectations of how the user will 'flow' through the app and the experience they will have. These wireframes will then be developed further when looking at user interface design and visual design, but this initial process will very much shape how the project develops. My favourite wireframing tool is Balsamiq Mockups. It's easy to use and allows you to create clickable wireframes very quickly: **http://www.balsamiq.com/products/mockups**.

As we are working through this specification process, there are a number of techniques we can use that will help make our initial plan as robust as possible and likely to succeed. We've already discussed these in depth in Chapter 9 on mobile sites, so it's worth taking a look at these if you haven't already, but I've summarized them below for quick reference:

Personas

Personas are fictional characters that try to encompass as many of the characteristics of the target audience as possible. Any set audience may encompass a number of different personas, and these personas can be created to varying levels of detail.

A basic persona may just include things like key needs, desires and motivators, whereas a very detailed persona may be given an elaborate background story including work details, family, personal values and demographics like age and location.

The aim of the persona is to give us something to test our mobile designs against and allows us to ask some key questions. Would the design we have suggested match the needs of this persona? How would the needs of different personas differ, and how does this impact our design?

Technical specification

You will also need to start considering technical aspects of your project at this stage as well. On which devices is it planned to work and what versions of these devices (iPhone 5 or 6, what about older versions etc)? How quickly should the app respond to user input? What versions of the operating system will it work on?

There are many questions at this stage that will lead to important decisions down the line, and many people with great ideas for apps don't know how to answer these questions so leave them unasked. This then means that the app developer will decide how these questions are answered, and this may not be in line with what you have planned. For this reason it is worth bringing a developer or someone with technical knowledge to help you define this stage of the project. Many see this early technical help as an unnecessary cost, but in my experience it can help you answer many questions early in the project before it gets expensive to change your mind.

Scenarios

Scenarios are imagined circumstances in which to place our personas and map out the key circumstances, needs and activities that may occur. This means that, as well as using the persona to understand individual needs, the scenario gives us the context. This can include things like physical location at a particular time, a set of circumstances or events, as well as external factors such as time pressures.

Use cases

A use case is a step-by-step description of the interaction between the persona and the mobile device/mobile site. This allows us to map how the device and mobile site will be interacted with, click by click. It also allows us to see the steps that are being taken by the persona and to understand how the flow of a particular task can be optimized.

By carrying out a robust specification process we will have made good progress in designing the information architecture (how the content fits together) and started to define the interaction design. We now need to define this interaction phase further and think about the other visual elements of the app.

Interaction and visual design

Once we have a clear view of the functionality and the fundamentals of our app we can start to consider the user interface in more detail and then consider the visual design. As we have discussed in Chapter 9, it is essential not to get too concerned with visual design too early in the project lifecycle. Although the visual elements of an app can be essential to its success, we need to get the core functionality right first. It is much easier to change visual design on top of a functional platform than it is to go back and fix the functionality.

I have divided the design phase into 'user interaction' design and 'visual' design for a number of reasons. Firstly, I consider these to be very distinct parts of the app. Although they must work effectively together, by focussing on the importance of the interaction design, we can achieve a more usable app. In an ideal world the app should need no instructions for use, as its interface should be so intuitive that the user should immediately understand its functionality and interface. This ease of interaction is the job of the interaction designer.

The visual design is the visual identity or 'skin' of the app. You may find a designer with expertise in both interaction and visual design. You may even feel that your app only requires an interaction designer, as functionality is key.

Technical development and testing

At this stage you have a well-thought-out app, with key functionality, interaction design and visual identity defined. You are now ready to hand your idea over to a developer. The better defined your idea is, the more likely it is that you will get the app that you have visualized. You must also remember at this stage that you may need to make changes and modifications to your original design based on what the developer thinks is possible and/or appropriate. This is why it pays to get a developer involved in the specification in the first place. It is also advisable to use a designer with experience in mobile app design on the particular operating system/s that you are planning on developing for.

We'll discuss in more detail the various operating systems and options you have when planning your app later, but your developer will clearly need skills in the particular approach you are taking. Also remember that many developers will be skilled in one approach but not necessarily the others, and if you are designing for multiple operating systems, you may need to use multiple developers.

You're going to need a developer to help you with testing, because until your app is in one of the app stores, you won't be able to get it into your phone without some technical assistance. There are a number of simulators that allow you to have a simulated device on your desktop, but these are never 100 per cent accurate and nothing beats real-world testing. Ideally, you need to test your app on as many devices and operating system versions as possible. In reality there are plenty of professional testers that can help with this process. You can use a freelancer or this may be a service that an agency offers as part of its overall service. We'll talk about freelancers and agencies more later.

The main reason for focussing your efforts on testing is that you need to meet certain criteria in order to be allowed to upload your app into the major app stores in the first place. Secondly, if you release an app with bugs and faults, you will upset the initial users, most likely get bad reviews and then get no more downloads. Invest the time to get it right the first time round.

App store submission

Submitting your app to the major app stores requires you to set up an account, agree that you have met the submission requirements and then to submit the appropriate file formats. This generally takes some technical knowledge so your first reaction may be to get your developer to do this for you. That approach is fine, but you need to make sure the account under which it is submitted belongs to you. This means you own the app and any profits it may make. It also means that you have control of the app for future changes. No problem having someone do this for you: but make sure everyone is clear on ownership and revenue.

The Apple App Store has a review process that can take some time. Most apps are reviewed within a number of days, but the process can take months if you are rejected for some reason and have to resubmit multiple times. This means you will need to have a clear view on final launch date and take into account review times after submission. The process on Google Play (Google's app store) is generally more straightforward, but you still need to make sure you are meeting their submission guidelines.

App marketing

It is very easy to create a fantastic app that gets hardly any downloads. For every success story, there are tens of thousands of apps that never get anywhere. The pure volume of apps means that you need to get visibility to stand a chance of achieving success. The more downloads your app gets, the more visibility it tends to get in the app stores, and in turn the more downloads you get. It's a virtuous circle once it gets going, but it's hard to get going in the first place.

App store algorithms

The visibility you get in the app stores is based on a number of factors, and these factors or rules make up the algorithms behind the charts.

There is a fair bit of complexity to these algorithms, but the core factors below decide whether you are at the top of the app charts and getting lots of visibility, or are nowhere to be seen:

- number of downloads;
- recency of these downloads;
- number of reviews;
- average star rating of reviews.

Based on this you want lots of downloads and positive reviews, concentrated over a period of time to get a boost up the charts. Clearly a well-thought-out marketing plan can help with this (as well as having a great app).

Outside the app stores

Although over 80 per cent of apps are found within the app stores (MobiMarketing, 2013), this approach is getting harder and harder, due to the huge volumes of apps being published. For this reason we need to make sure we are leveraging our other channels to drive app downloads. This can include promotion via social media sites (which we'll explore more in Chapter 13 on mobile advertising) as well as creating app landing pages. These landing pages can form part of our website and can drive increased downloads via cross-promotion and discovery via search engines. A novel use of SMS messaging is to use a website landing page to offer the service of sending an SMS to a mobile device in order to make the app download easy. We'll look at this option more in Chapter 17 on SMS.

Social media sharing and interaction

Make sure that you make it as easy and as likely as possible that a user will share your app via social media. Social sharing options within apps can work well, particularly when the user is rewarded in some way for sharing. This reward could be by highlighting an achievement within an app, or by giving extra rewards in exchange for sharing.

Gamification

Gamification is the principle of encouraging behaviours by rewarding a user in some way. This may be as simple as posting a high score to a public leader board (and remember this doesn't need to be limited to games, it could be for the most technical questions answered etc). It can take more complex forms, such as being the first user to discover a piece of hidden content, or unlocking hidden features when certain activities are carried out.

The key thing that makes gamification work is that the reward should be valuable to the user. This may be in the form of content or reward, and very often that reward can just be recognition.

For my favourite example of gamification, take a look at the video for Jay-Z's *Decoded* book launch: http://www.youtube.com/watch?v=XNic4wf8AYg.

Another social media consideration is where you will interact and get feedback from your app users. The app stores can allow this in a limited way, but social platforms allow you to get more detailed feedback and to build engagement and advocacy with your audience.

App maintenance

Once your app is fully tested and live in the app store/s, you may think that your development requirements are fulfilled. In fact there are two key reasons why you are going to need to keep on developing your app.

The first is user feedback. If you want to grow your downloads you need to keep improving things, reacting to user feedback and creating a better app. This will give you the opportunity to engage with your audience as well as differentiate yourself from the competition. Changes and updates give you something to talk about and can drive interest in your app. This also indicates to potential downloaders that your app is well maintained and can encourage more downloads. There are also a whole host of app developers who take existing ideas, improve them and then release these apps into the market. In order to stay ahead of this approach, you need to keep developing and refining your ideas.

Another reason that you will need to consider maintenance is the release of new phones and operating systems. As a new version of a phone, new device or new operating system is released, you are going to need to make sure your app is working properly. A bug caused by a new operating system or device can lead to bad reviews, and this can kill a previously successful app.

Customer support

Just as with any product or service, you need to look after your customers. Even for free apps, it's essential to react to feedback and fix bugs. This will help you reduce poor feedback and get the positive reviews that will encourage downloads and move you up the app charts.

Freelancers vs agencies

If you don't have the skills personally or inside your organization to create your app, you're going to need to find the skills elsewhere. You're going to need to understand the different options available to you in bringing in those necessary skills. First of all, here are the main differences between working with an agency and a freelancer.

Freelancers

Freelancers are generally the cheapest option (although some very experienced high quality freelancers may be the same price as an agency). With a freelancer you are dealing with an individual – this in itself can have pros and cons. You are talking directly to the person doing the work so there is no incorrect channelling of communications or messages getting lost between people. It also means that if your freelancer is on holiday, off sick, or down the pub, there is nobody to speak to. They also generally won't have a finance or admin team and they probably won't have an office. This means meetings will happen at your premises or in a public place such as a cafe. This is a nice idea in theory but being surrounded by other people when you are discussing your top secret plan for launching the next Facebook or Twitter isn't ideal (although the coffee is often good). It's also unlikely you'll be their only client, so you need assurances in regard to how much of their time you are getting and their availability for discussing and feeding back on a particular project. All this aside, working with a freelancer can be very cost effective, and if you pick your freelancer well, the work can be excellent.

Agencies

Agencies will tend to have better facilities, including a range of staff for different tasks. This means there will generally be somebody to speak to when you need to – but don't make any assumptions about this and make sure you get an SLA (service level agreement) that guarantees availability, turnaround time, etc). One of the great joys of working with an agency (or pitfalls when it's not working properly) is your account manager. An account manager will be your first point of contact within a mid- to large size agency (many agencies don't have account managers, particularly the smaller ones) and is generally responsible for channelling your requests to the right member of the team, getting feedback and reports for you, and generally fighting your side within the agency. This is great if you have a good account manager with whom you get on well. If you don't, it's a recipe for disaster as your main point of contact and communications channel will essentially be broken. Make sure you meet your account manager before signing a contract, and ask to speak to another client that has worked with the agency and has used the same account manager.

Agencies can be anything from a couple of freelancers working together to multinational companies with dozens of offices worldwide and teams of staff in the hundreds/thousands. Correspondingly, they can offer very different levels of service.

Questions to ask

The following are some of the key things you should check before you commit to engaging agencies or freelancers:

- **Have they worked on exactly this kind of project before?** A lot of us like challenges and interesting work, but do you really want to pay for your supplier's learning curve? Although if you doing something truly original there will be some learning to do.

- **Who specifically will be working on the project and what is their experience?** Very often you meet the top consultant but they won't actually be doing the work. I always struggled with this when I worked in the agency environment as I would be pitching the work but somebody else would be delivering it. This meant a project that was signed on the basis of my communication and relationship with someone delivering on the promises I made – all fine when it works but can be difficult when it doesn't. The solution to this is clear and structured briefings and clarity early on about who is doing what.

- **Are they just pushing the work out to a freelancer themselves and marking up the cost?** Although this can also work if they are adding value in terms of project management, communication and quality control.

- **Will they need to interact with other suppliers and are they experienced in doing this?** Ask to see examples of whom they have worked with on what work. This most often happens when design and development is done by different companies/individuals. My best advice on this is to assign a lead agency/freelancer who is responsible for the overall project. This means they must make sure all parties have the correct communications, adhere to deadlines and attend the relevant meetings. This will save you a lot of administrative work as well making someone responsible for ensuring everyone knows what is going on.

- **How much are they willing to do to pitch for your work?**
  An individual or company that goes the extra mile in the
  pitch is hungry for the work and will generally pay you more
  attention when you are a client. By the extra mile, I mean the
  pitch you receive should not be generic.

- **What happens if you can't agree on design?** The problem with
  design work is that it can be subjective in part, so discuss what
  will happen if, after you have signed up, they can't come up
  with a design that you like. Generally the agreement you sign
  will offer you a number of design concepts to choose from.
  Make sure this is clear, and then see how much the design of
  choice can be tweaked and changed. Is this limited in the
  contract? You can find yourself in an endless loop of design
  tweaks that lead to a very average design. Choose a designer
  who has produced work you like, has studied design
  professionally and thoroughly understands usability – then let
  them do their job. Unfortunately most designs are ruined by
  one of two things: they were no good in the first place, or they
  started off well and then one or more people on the client side
  made changes until there was nothing interesting left. If there
  is no one in your organization (whether you or someone else)
  with a professional understanding of design, then don't act as
  if there is! It's amazing how many MDs and CEOs feel they are
  experts in web design!

- **What are the timescales? What happens if the agency/
  freelancer misses their deadlines? What are your
  responsibilities and when do they need to be delivered?
  What happens if you miss your deadlines?** I generally look to
  add a clause to any contract that gives you a discount if the
  supplier misses the deadline by more than an agreed amount.
  This will depend on you signing things off and providing
  content at the appropriate time but it serves to make sure
  the supplier sets a realistic schedule in the first place.

Finding agencies and freelancers

The best way to find an agency in my opinion is via personal recommendation. Social networks make this increasingly easy to do and it's my favourite use of LinkedIn. If you don't have direct social connections with experience in the right type of work, look at options like LinkedIn groups. There are many very active digital marketing discussion groups where you should be able to get several opinions. My general experience is that you need to find the balance between an agency that is big enough to service your needs but is small enough to be hungry for your work. It's never good being a small client for a big agency.

Finding freelancers has become increasingly easy thanks to great websites like Elance. These sites allow you to set your requirements and the freelancers to pitch for your work. You can review their previous work, feedback from other clients, and see how many jobs they have completed, along with average feedback ratings. I love Elance and have built relationships with several developers around the world that I use for all of my development projects now.

Native apps vs web apps

Let's start by discussing some key options we have when approaching the development of an app. A 'native app' is one that is developed for a specific mobile platform, such as iOS for Apple devices or Android-powered devices. We've taken a look at the adoption levels of these devices in various global markets in Part One of this book, and we'll explore the various platforms further in a moment. The key thing to understand is that when you are building an app in this way, you need to develop a different version of the app for each platform.

Web apps, however, have the advantage that they will work on any mobile device that has a suitable browser and language support. Web apps are generally created using HTML5, and the majority of smartphones and tablets support HTML5 apps. So on initial inspection we may think that the obvious choice is a web app, as we only need to create one version. Unfortunately, it definitely isn't that simple and there are quite a few factors to consider.

Web connection

Firstly, web apps very often rely on having some form of internet connection. It is possible to create web apps that give functionality when disconnected from the web; however, this doesn't have the same level of flexibility that native apps can achieve. Don't forget though, that plenty of native apps like Google Maps also require an internet connection to function properly.

Device functionality

Increasingly, web apps are able to utilize lots of the mobile device features we take for granted in native apps, like geographic location and things like access to cameras. However, this varies from platform to platform, the device being used and the browser on that device. This makes things a little more limited and complex on web apps.

Performance

Native apps offer better performance, speed and a smoother user experience generally. This makes them much better suited to apps that need fast graphics processing or screen swiping. For this reason, there aren't that many successful web app-based games.

Cost

Web apps are generally a lot cheaper to produce than web apps. The development process is easier and you don't have a submissions process as with the native platforms.

Security

Native apps are generally more secure than web apps, due to the control and procedures put in place by the main app stores. This also means that users see these stores as more trustworthy. Users are also less familiar with web apps and therefore have built less trust in this approach.

Monetization

The app stores make it easy to sell your apps and there are various advertising and subscription options available as standard. Therefore native apps are generally easier to monetize. Web apps need to rely on taking payment in similar ways to a website, and this adds a barrier to payment as users very often will not want to enter credit card details into an app, or may not be willing to use a third-party payment system like PayPal, because of a lack of trust in the web app.

Updates and maintenance

It is much easier to update and maintain a web app, as there is no store you need to submit to, and development is generally quicker and easier than for native apps.

In conclusion, web apps offer some great advantages in terms of development costs and speed to market. They also have the distinct advantage of creating an app once for delivery on multiple platforms. However, these advantages are often out-weighed by the disadvantages and limitations of what can currently be achieved with a web app. As mobile browsers and operating systems grow in sophistication, this may change, as the lines between native and web apps begin to blur.

Platform wars

We are going to look at key differences between the two core mobile platforms: iOS from Apple, and Android from Google and their app stores. As discussed earlier in Part One of this book, there are other mobile operating systems such as Symbian, Blackberry and Windows Mobile, but the reality is that you need to have a very specific target audience in mind if you are developing for these relatively low adoption platforms. That last sentence will cause outrage in some quarters, but realistically, when over 95 per cent of global smartphone and tablet operating system market share (MobiThinking, 2013) is held by these two platforms, you need to have a very good justification to look elsewhere.

> ### Latest app platform statistics
>
> We've explored adoption of these various platforms in Chapter 6 on mobile statistics, but you can of course get the latest stats on our website as well: http://www.targetinternet.com/mobilemarketing.

Apple has its App Store and Google has Google Play, the name it now uses for where you can buy and download all forms of content, including apps (as well as music, movies etc). Both app stores and platforms have a lot of similarities, but there are also some key differences.

The iOS operating system and the Apple App Store are owned, controlled and developed solely by Apple. This means they call the shots. Android, although owned by Google, is actually distributed as an open source platform, meaning it can theoretically be used and adapted by anyone. It's also been adopted by the Open Handset Alliance (OHA) which includes big handset manufacturers like Samsung, Sony and HTC.

When you design an app for iOS, you are designing two key formats: an iPhone and a iPad version (which currently come in two flavours, mini and standard size). When you design and develop for Android devices it's not that straightforward, and in reality your app could be used on any number of differently sized devices. For this reason, you need to make sure your Android developer is experienced in thinking this process through carefully, especially when the range of Android devices is growing so quickly.

The other key difference between the app stores is the submission process. On the Android platform, as long as you meet the guidelines and go through the appropriate processes, you can quite quickly have your app live on Play. However, with the Apple App Store, you have to go through a manual approval process. This can take anything from a few days though to months when things go wrong. In my experience, about 5–10 days is average. The manual reviewers are not only looking for any deviation from the guidelines given by Apple, but also for any bugs or poor user experience. They are also thorough and pretty fussy. This makes a better user experience, but can be frustrating for a new app creator. Always remember, it's better that any issues get identified now rather than by a real user, which in turn could attract negative reviews and kill your app.

Building an app: conclusions

Before you embark on creating your first app, make sure you understand the process and skills involved. Make sure the user experience is second to none, and test your app thoroughly. Always remember that even a great app won't get any traction without great marketing (or a huge amount of luck) and that you need to focus on supporting your app users to get great reviews.

It can be a complicated and frustrating process at times, but there aren't many things as satisfying as seeing your app climb up the app store charts. Good luck!

> I'm always fascinated to hear about people's successes and failures in the app world. Tell us about what you've learnt and achieved and we may feature your app on our site and give you that marketing boost you need: **http://www.targetinternet.com/mobilemarketing**.

11 Social media and mobile

The reality is that, other than browsing the web, we spend more time using social media than any other activity on our smartphones (*Telegraph*, 2013). Social media also only comes second to games when we consider what we are using mobile apps for (Flurry Analytics, 2013).

Mobile devices allow us to capture and share our experiences, connect our real-world experiences to our online world and to stay up to date with what's going on around us. Therefore, mobile devices are intrinsically social, and this is why social media is such an important aspect of mobile. Our mobile devices represent the bridge between our real-world lives and our online interactions. This means that social media via mobile devices offers huge potential.

What we need to consider is how to best utilize this social behaviour for our organizations and to help achieve our business objectives without interrupting an individual's private and personal space. Over 76 per cent of Facebook users are at least 'slightly concerned' about privacy issues (Statista, 2013), which indicates the general awareness of how all of the data we share via social media carries some risks.

User journey and value proposition

Two of the main themes that we discussed in the first section of this book were understanding the user journey and considering our value proposition. These considerations are key to using social media effectively. We need to make sure we understand which social platforms my target audience are using and make sure that when they use these platforms the mobile user experience is fully optimized. We also need to make sure we are providing value via social media and not just posting for the sake of posting.

Content and engagement

Just like all social media, our ability to utilize it effectively will come down to having interesting and useful content to share, and being willing and able to engage in an open and 'non-corporate' way. Because of the personal nature of mobile devices and of social media, a standard 'corporate communications' tone doesn't work. Even in a B2B environment, we are still dealing with individuals and need to apply core social media principles to our communications.

Bear in mind that anybody can blog, post to social media sites and tweet. In fact many best practice guides say you should tweet around four times a day for maximum impact (Adobe, 2013). You should only do any of these things though, if you have something interesting to say.

Mobile social media experience

We need to consider the fact that the majority of people using social media on mobile devices are using apps to access these platforms (we've looked at apps in more detail in the previous chapter). I personally use the Facebook, Twitter, Google+ and LinkedIn apps on my iPhone every day. So what does this particular way of accessing social media mean in terms of our mobile marketing? It means that we need to think in terms of accessing our content via the constraints of these apps.

For example, if you post content to Twitter (or Weibo sites in China), most of the time you will be sharing a link. How does that link display on a mobile device? With over 60 per cent of Twitter users accessing the service via mobile devices (Marketing Land, 2013), we need to consider the mobile experience of the links we are driving people to. My own tweets split into two core categories: linking to useful content on my site; and linking to useful content on other people's sites. I know that the experience on my site has been fully optimized for mobile users, but is this the case for other sites I am driving people through to?

Another example is using social networks like Facebook and LinkedIn. Generally in this case we are posting content to try and create engagement, and very often this content will include images. The images may display very well on a desktop size screen, but how do they look on a mobile? Much of the social network experience is different in a mobile app as opposed to a desktop version. We need to make sure we have considered this in all of our social posts. We have to assume that users will be on a mobile device at some point and therefore make sure everything works in this format.

Social media in China

If you are targeting the huge potential of the Chinese market, or you are working within China, you need to be aware (or probably already are) that social media can, at first sight, look very different to elsewhere in the world. Actually the core principles of content, engagement and transparency all still apply, but you will find yourself using completely different platforms.

In most countries globally the social media platforms are fairly universal (with a few exceptions like Mixi in Japan or VK in Russia), but in China there is no Twitter, Facebook or YouTube. Instead there are local market equivalents. RenRen and PengYou are social networks similar to Facebook. Weibo's are microblogs like Twitter and there are several, including Sina Weibo and Tencent Weibo. QQ is the most popular instant messenger and Youku is a popular equivalent to YouTube.

Just as with any market, you need to understand what social platforms your target audience is using and then engage using the right tone and content.

For a great resource on social media in China, and the whole Asia region, take a look at: **http://www.techinasia.com/**.

Informing your social media approach

There are a number of tools that can help inform and manage our social media activity and make sure we are delivering the right content in the right way.

Using search to inform content themes

Google Trends is a fantastic free tool that allows us to see how users search in Google and the trends in searches over time. The great thing about this tool is that not only can we understand search trends but we can use this to inform our social content. We look at this tool a lot more in Chapter 12 on mobile search, but in this case we are going to use it find out what people are interested in, in order to inform what we should be talking about on our social platforms. The chart in Figure 11.1 shows searches for the word 'iPhone' over a particular period of time: **http://www.google.co.uk/trends**.

The standard Trends tool will show you relative search volumes over time for a particular word or phrase. We can drill down by time, region, country or language. The tool will try and identify related news stories to points on the graph, showing us geographical interest and the most popular and fastest rising variations of these search terms.

Probably the most important feature is the ability to compare the trends for different search terms, and this is particularly important for informing content.

Figure 11.2 shows the phrases 'internet marketing' and 'digital marketing' being compared. We can see a decline in interest for internet marketing and a rise in interest for digital marketing. I clearly need to be talking about digital marketing rather than internet marketing on my social platform, because that's what people are searching for and are interested in.

One thing to be clear about is that Google Trends shows you relative volumes of searches, not the actual numbers of searches. If you want the actual number of searches, you'll need to use the Keyword Tool, and we discuss this in Chapter 12 on mobile search. Relative volumes will show a score of 100 at the peak volume of searches.

FIGURE 11.1   Google Trends: search for the word 'iPhone'
(www.google.com/trends)

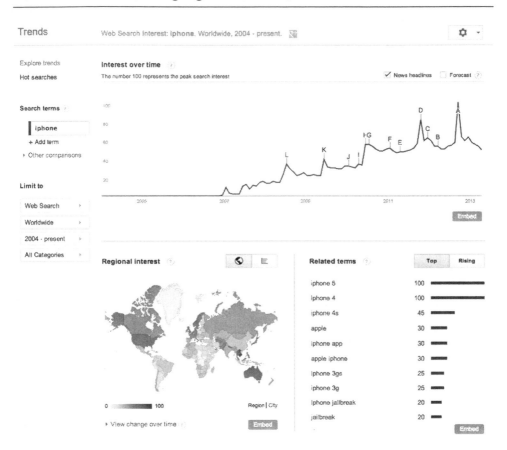

The rest of the score over time is relative to this. When multiple words are compared, the highest point with a 100 score is the most searched of the words being compared at its highest search volume.

One of the limitations of the Trends tool is its lack of ability to show trends for niche search terms. You'll find in many cases that a niche search term shows that it doesn't have enough data to plot a chart.

Social listening tools

Social listening tools are something that every organization of every size should be using. They allow you to monitor a number of different social channels to look for activity around certain phrases or topics.

FIGURE 11.2 Google Trends: word comparison
(www.google.com/trends)

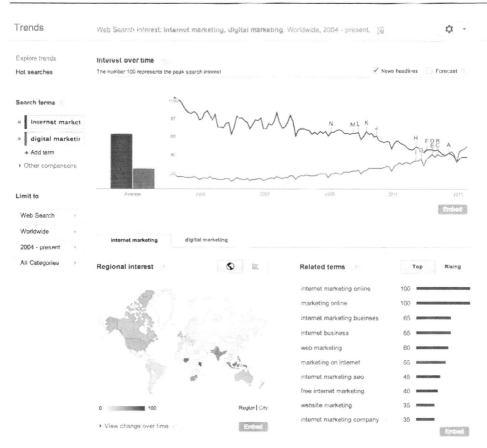

This capability can be used at a number of stages throughout social media campaigns and these listening tools are essential for effective social media use.

Firstly, these tools can be used in the 'listening' stage, when we are trying to understand what social channels our audience are using, what they are saying, what they are interested in and what our competitors are doing. Many organizations will carry out a listening project before starting any social media activity as part of their standard process before initiating a campaign.

Next, these tools can be used to monitor the effectiveness of social media activity. We can monitor groups of words and phrases to see what is happening on an ongoing basis, and how our audience reacts to our social activity.

Finally, social listening tools can be used to manage outreach and engagement, by identifying key influencers on social channels. This can be important when trying to grow your audience, but also when dealing with negative feedback or a crisis. The idea is to influence the influencers, much like in traditional PR, but in the case of social media we can do this at a much more granular level.

Some social listening tools also include elements of workflow management, and help you to manage your social media efforts. For example, you may be able to track which social media users you have engaged with, which individual in your organization was involved and plan future activities.

Social media monitoring and listening tools

There is a huge array of social media monitoring tools out there, varying widely in price and capability. At the free end of the spectrum you'll find an enormous selection of tools. However, these tools are fairly limited, and the old adage that you get what you pay for generally holds true. It's worth checking out SocialMention.com and Addictomatic.com (not really a social listening tool, but it can be helpful) for examples of what you can get.

The number of paid-for tools available is dizzying, but I would certainly recommend the following:

- **http://www.viralheat.com** – low cost and practical social monitoring. I use this one daily.

- **http://www.brandwatch.com** – my favourite social monitoring tool and well worth the cost. Very powerful, flexible and used by some of the world's leading companies.

- **http://www.sproutsocial.com** – another great tool at a reasonable cost with some great management features.

- **http://www.salesforcemarketingcloud.com** – Radian6 is owned by Salesforce, the cloud-based CRM platform. Powerful and suited to very large brands due to its pricing.

You can find a list of even more tools on our website: **http://www.targetinternet.com/mobilemarketing/**.

Social analysis tools

Social analysis tools are different to social listening/monitoring tools in that they generally look at one social platform and give you some analysis or functionality for that particular platform. In fact many social media sites have these built in. For example, Facebook Insights will give you a range of reports that allow you to see which of your posts were most popular, where the users that like you are in the world, and who is engaging with your content.

There are literally thousands of these tools out there but I have highlighted a few below to give you a flavour of what you can expect. Generally they will analyse your audience and content and give you some insight into how to take your campaigns forward:

- **http://www.tweriod.com** – find out the most effective time of day and day of the week to post your tweets.

- **http://twtrland.com/** – analyse your Twitter audience with this excellent free tool.

- **http://www.storify.com** – collate social media content on a topic into story.

- Facebook Insights – accessed when you have set up a Facebook page, Insights gives you huge insight into what content is working.

- YouTube Insights – another one accessed via the social platform itself, to find out which of your videos are actually getting engagement.

- **http://www.followerwonk.com** – oddly named and very powerful tool for analysing Twitter audiences and growing your audience.

Figure 11.3 shows an example of the many social analysis tools out there (and one of my favourites): twtrland.com analysing my Twitter account.

The list could go on and on, so we've compiled and are constantly updating a huge list on the website to accompany this book: **http://www.targetinternet.com**.

FIGURE 11.3   Analysis of a Twitter account using twtrland.com (www.twtrland.com)

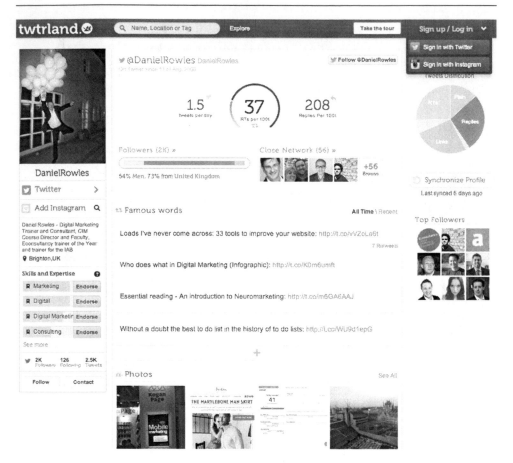

Analytics

Your web analytics is one of the most powerful tools for informing your social media activity. You'll not only be able to understand which social media sites are driving traffic to your website, but also how many of these visitors were on mobile devices, and which devices they were.

We'll explore analytics in a great deal more detail in Chapter 18 on mobile analytics, but it is worth mentioning at this point that analytics can help you understand the impact of your social media campaigns on your broader digital objectives.

> ### The importance of Google Analytics
>
> Google Analytics is a powerful and sophisticated web analytics platform that also happens to be free. It has around 82 per cent market share of the entire analytics market (Techcrunch, 2013) and is improving and offering more and more functionality all of the time. It is suitable for the majority of site owners' needs and offers extensive reports around mobile sites and apps.
>
> There are of course other commercial analytics packages available, and these have the advantage of account managers and service level agreements. Google Analytics Premium does offer these things, but pricing is currently $150,000 annually.

Real-world integration

Remember, that if you want a mobile user to find and engage with you via social media, you need to make it easy for them to do so. You can rely on a number of sources to drive users to your social sites, but don't forget those who are doing things offline. Make sure you use things like QR codes, NFC and easily typed-in URLs to drive people to your social sites. Also, don't forget to consider the visibility of your social platforms in mobile search, and make sure that your social activity can be found from your mobile sites.

It's also worth trying to drive visitors to share any content they may be experiencing via a mobile device. Adding sharing buttons can be effective, but make sure they don't clutter the limited real estate available on mobile devices. Also don't forget to test the sharing experience on different mobile platforms. Just because it works on the desktop version, doesn't mean it will on mobile.

Policy and planning

So you have worked out the kind of content you are going to need and you understand which channels are appropriate for your target audience. You've also thought through the mobile experience and made sure that it is optimized at all stages. You are ready to start your mobile social media activity? Nope. One of the most important elements of successful social media is having a clear and workable social media policy, and this should have specific considerations for mobile devices.

Social media policies are there to help anyone involved in carrying out your social activity and outline the do's and don'ts of social media within your organization. They will outline things like those listed below:

- reporting structure of team involved with social media and clear direction where to seek advice;
- appropriate social media channels;
- guidance on tone of voice;
- guidance on suggested tools, log-ins and who should be using them;
- process for identification and mitigation of risks;
- escalation policy for use when problems are identified;
- responsibilities and legal requirements;
- guidance on suitable content;
- direction on frequency of content posting;
- moderation guidelines;
- best practice on posting mobile-optimized content;
- guidance on creating mobile-optimized landing pages;
- mobile testing platforms;
- guide to success measures and relevant analytics reports.

Every organization should have its own social media policy and this can help mitigate risks, create effective and consistent social communications and make sure that everyone understands the importance of mobile-optimized content.

> ### Database of social media policies
>
> This site has a huge list of example social media policies you can review to provide insights for your own site. At the time of publishing there were over 200 policies listed: **http://socialmediagovernance.com/policies.php**.

Outreach, engagement and ego

Although this is not something that is exclusive to mobile social media, we should always consider how we can maximize our reach into our target audience. Social outreach and engagement is a highly effective way of doing this, and as well as increasing the size of our audience it can help us create positive engagement as well.

If I keep on publishing useful and engaging content, regularly update my social channels and positively engage with anyone who leaves comments or feedback, I will gradually grow my social media audience. If, however, I want to speed up this process and create the maximum amplification for my efforts, I am going to need to focus on social media outreach.

Social outreach is all about identifying the key influencers and advocates within a particular group. If I can get these key people to share my updates and content I can amplify my visibility and potentially grow my audience.

So let's define what we mean by an influencer or an advocate:

- **Advocates** are the easiest group to identify as they are those people who leave positive comments, re-tweet things and generally engage in a positive way. They are willing to spread what you say and add to your social voice. They are our greatest asset and we need to engage, encourage and reward this group to build loyalty.

- **Influencers** are those people with access to the audience we want to influence. We can use social media tools to identify them and we then need a strategy to get engagement and encourage them to become advocates.

Judging influence

You can use a number of measures to judge influence online. You could look at the number of social connections somebody has, or look at the quality of their audience. You could consider how likely it is that what they say will be read and repeated. This process can be quite time-consuming and therefore it is worth considering some of the key tools that can help us understand influence.

FIGURE 11.4   Klout: social media influence scoring platform (www.klout.com)

Klout, pictured in Figure 11.4, aims to take the pain away from trying to work out influence online. It works by looking at a range of social platforms, assessing over 400 different factors, such as your likelihood of being retweeted, and then gives you a score out of 100. It will also assign topics it believes you are influential about. So from the screenshot above you can see I currently have a score of 62 and according to Klout I am influential about social media, mobile marketing and digital marketing (phew!).

Scoring services such as Klout have actually received a lot of negative press and have been accused of everything from inaccuracy through to being nothing more than a way of flattering people's egos. I disagree. Although Klout is far from perfect, as their algorithm (the set of rules behind the scores) improves, so does its effectiveness. There will always be arguments about how much a particular factor or platform should be weighted, but in reality it can give you the rough guidance you need. If I look at all of my Twitter followers and look at those with the highest Klout scores, there is no doubt that these people are my most influential audience.

The key point of Klout is that it gives me a simple metric to initially assess online influence (of an individual or an organization). I can then dig a little deeper and plan my campaigns to reach out to these online influencers. For example, I have a plugin for Google Chrome that shows me the Klout score of all the people whose tweets I am reading on Twitter. That way I can see who is most influential and prioritize my engagement activities.

There are other social influence tools out there; you may also want to take a look at **http://www.kred.com** and some of the Twitter analysis tools we have already mentioned can be useful for this as well.

FIGURE 11.5   Influential Twitter users on the topic of SEO
(www.viralheat.com)

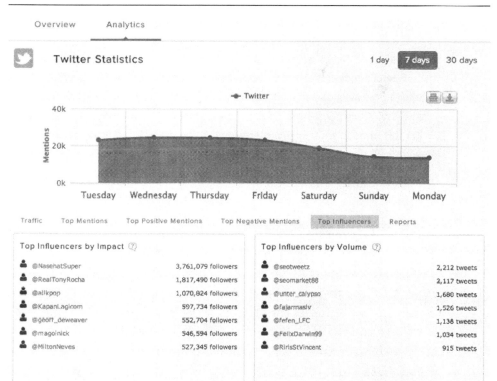

Another approach to judging social influence is to use a social monitoring tool that helps you identify the most influential users on a particular platform. The screen shot in Figure 11.5 is taken from the ViralHeat social media listening tool that we mentioned earlier in this chapter. This screen shot shows two groups of potentially influential users on the topic of 'SEO' (search engine optimization). It shows those people that have tweeted the most on this topic in the last seven days and those people that have tweeted about SEO but also have the most followers. I can then reach out to these people and find some way to engage with them and build some form of relationship.

Social media, online PR and search optimization

It's important to understand that there is a very close connection between your social media activity, public relations (PR) activity and search optimization. We'll look at mobile search in more detail in the next chapter, but the effectiveness of your social media activity will create 'social signals' that influence your search rankings (essentially the quantity and quality of conversation that is happening in social media around your topics of interest).

Social engagement and outreach are essentially online PR, but your offline PR activities can also impact what you talk about in social media and how many people are linking to your sites and social media platforms. For this reason, we need everyone involved in these three disciplines to work collaboratively and be aware of what the others are doing.

Social measurement

The greatest mistake made in a huge number of organizations (in my experience the majority) is to focus on volume-based metrics when looking at social media campaigns. More often than not, a campaign is started and the initial target is to reach a certain number of likes or followers. But in reality what does having a million followers actually mean? The answer is very little. We need to understand who that audience are, look at how engaged they are, their sentiments, and, most importantly, understand if social media is actually having an impact on my business objectives.

We'll look at mobile analytics much more in the final chapter of Part Two, but we can use analytics to look at the success of our mobile social media activity in a number of ways. We can start with the basics, and look at how much traffic we are getting from social media sites to our websites. We could then take it a stage further and look at how many of these visits are on mobile devices. If we are using analytics effectively, we will have also set up goals, and we can see what part social media, and particularly mobile social media, is having on driving my website visitors to complete my goals. All of this will be covered in more detail in Chapter 18, but the key point is that it's not just about the social media data, like number of followers or amount of engagement: it's actually about understanding how this drives my end objectives.

Benchmarked measurement

One of the key problems with looking at volume-based metrics is that it doesn't give you an indication of what success actually looks like. You may feel that getting 10,000 followers on your Facebook page is a great success. However, if your nearest competitor has 500,000 followers, it's suddenly a very different story. For this reason we need to try and benchmark our measurement, and there are a couple of ratio-based measures that are easy to use, but very rarely looked at.

Share of voice

This is a great ratio for understanding where you sit in relation to your competitors, and for judging the success of and reaction to your social media efforts. You'll need a social media listening tool to calculate this, and for many channels there are free tools that will do the job.

You start by measuring the total level of conversation around the topic area you are concerned with. In my case this would be digital marketing, but it could be anything. For example, a recent client looked at all of the conversations around skincare. The easiest way to do this is to look at channels one at a time, so for example, how many tweets are there around the topic of skincare within a particular geographic region (you can do this using the Twitter advanced search).

You achieve this by deciding on a set of keywords and phrases that you want to monitor, and then see the level of conversation on these phrases. You would then repeat this process, but just identify the tweets that were specifically about, or mentioned, your product, brand or service. You will then have two numbers, one for total conversations and the other for conversations about you. Divide the number of conversations about you by the total number of conversations on the topic, and you have your 'share of voice' percentage.

This may be very low, but you can continue your social media efforts, and then take the measurement on a regular basis (normally monthly is sufficient). Progress made in increasing this percentage gives you a more useful guide than just looking at a number of tweets or likes. The other great thing about this measure is that you can calculate it for your competitors. You then have a benchmarked measure that can give you an indication of how effective your efforts are and how that compares to your competitors.

Sentiment analysis

Many social media tools will carry out some form of sentiment analysis. The idea is that the context of the social media mentions you receive is analysed, and the sentiment or intention of the social media user is understood. This most usually takes the form of grouping these mentions into positive, negative and neutral.

There is a problem however. The majority of social media tools get this completely wrong. These tools work by analysing the text and using fairly rudimentary methods of analysing the language. For example, if I tweet 'Top 10 digital marketing disasters of 2014' and then link to my website, many tools will see this as a negative tweet and associate negativity with the link to my website. It will be seen as negative due to the use of the word 'disaster'; however, from experience, this will actually be a very popular tweet. Some tools, however, are a lot more effective at analysing language and take a far more sophisticated approach. These tools certainly aren't 100 per cent accurate, but they are far less likely to make rudimentary mistakes like this.

The solution is to understand how effective your particular tool is at analysing the social platforms you are looking at, and then manually checking the results you get. This doesn't mean reading every single tweet or comment (although in an ideal world you will), but it certainly means scanning through and understanding the assumption the tool is making.

This is particularly important when you look at share of voice. During a really bad social media crisis, when everybody is talking about you and saying negative things, your share of voice will be high. You therefore need to understand sentiment when you look at share of voice.

Audience engagement

This is another percentage that you can easily measure and benchmark against your competitors. I tend to look at it on a platform-by-platform basis, so I will know my audience engagement for Twitter, Facebook, Google+ etc and make efforts to improve this. Again, I normally measure this on a monthly basis.

You start by looking at the size of your overall audience on a particular social platform, such as Facebook or Twitter, and then you consider how much of that audience is actually engaging with you. So, for example, if you have 10,000 likes in Facebook, and when you post some content you get 1,000 likes on that piece of content from your likes, your audience engagement is 10 per cent.

We need to define what we mean by engagement. On a platform such as Facebook, there are multiple ways to engage as you can like, share and comment on a post. I would count any of these activities as engagement. With Twitter I consider a reply or a retweet to be engagement, and so on. Now, technically speaking, if the same user were to carry out multiple engagement activities on the same platform on the same piece of content, we should probably not count these more than once. In practice it doesn't actually matter, as long as you are comparing like for like.

As well as taking this measure for your own social platforms, you can very easily analyse your competitors as well.

Benchmarking and business results

Although these benchmarked measures don't relate directly to business results, they are far more connected to helping us achieve our objectives than just looking at volume-based metrics alone. Realistically, if you are targeting the right audience, your share of voice is growing and your audience engagement is increasing, you are in a strong position.

The next stage is to connect these social media measures to our web analytics and business objectives, and we'll look at this in detail in Chapter 18 on Mobile Analytics.

Social media advertising

Many social media platforms give you a number of paid advertising options. Major search engines like Google, Yandex and Baidu also allow you to run paid search campaigns, which we will discuss in more depth in Chapter 12 on mobile search. We should discuss the implications of paid social campaigns here, however, as they can heavily impact the effectiveness and measurement of your social campaigns.

Facebook posted an increase in profits in the first quarter of 2013, up by 30 per cent from the previous quarter, and much of this was attributed to mobile advertising, with at least one third of this income from mobile advertising revenue. In the same announcement, Facebook said that 751 million of its 1.1 billion users are accessing Facebook every month on their mobile device (Sky, 2013). This increase in revenue via mobile is very much in line with our expectations of mobile growth, and everything we are discussing in this book, but it also offers some key challenges to consider.

Value proposition, privacy and trust

Since our mobile devices are in many cases very much part of our personal and social lives, we need to be very cautious about how we use these devices in a blatantly commercial way. Nearly everything we have spoken about so far involves providing value via engagement and understanding the user needs. Exactly the same principle should be applied to social advertising.

We need to consider how much of an interruption social advertising can actually be seen as, how it can actually damage our brands if used badly and what image we are projecting of our organization. Facebook themselves are responding to this, and already there are signs that users will be able to opt out of most ads on mobile devices if they wish to (Atlantic Wire, 2013).

The key point is to understand the social platforms you are using, why a user is there and make sure the value proposition is clear. If you are on Facebook, you are interested in health and fitness, and brands like Nike offer you free tools to help you achieve your fitness goals, then that's great. If, however, you are on Facebook and you have liked a digital marketing podcast, it doesn't mean that any of your friends necessarily have an interest (see the example below).

FIGURE 11.6   Facebook Insights: the impact on audience size of promoting a post (www.facebook.com)

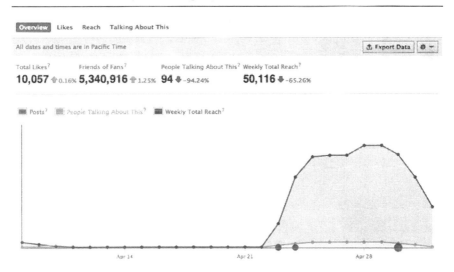

The screen shot in Figure 11.6 shows how much of an impact running a promotion on a post in Facebook can have on boosting your audience. In this particular case, the sharp rise in audience and engagement, shown by the steep rise in the graph, was caused by promoting a post. Promoting posts will make your post more visible to those people that have already liked you, but it also means that your post is shown to the friends of your likes as well. Whilst in this particular case this leads to an increase in overall likes and engagement (as well as a knock-on impact in Klout score), what isn't clear is how many people saw my ad for whom it wasn't relevant, and how much of an impact this had on what these people thought of my brand. The problem is there is no way of finding out who these people are and what impact these ads have had on them.

Trusting algorithms

The reality is that it's actually in Facebook's interest not to annoy people with irrelevant ads, just as it's not good for Google to give you irrelevant search results. Both scenarios lead to dissatisfied users, which in turn leads to those users moving to other social networks and search engines. The problem is that Facebook is under serious pressure (*Telegraph*, 2013) to increase its profits but it can't do this at the expense of losing users.

The algorithms, which are just sets of rules and logic, behind these sites are what decide which ads you are shown or which search results you are given. Google has spent many years and much investment in developing its algorithms and focussing on relevancy. For Facebook it's relatively early days, and mobile advertising for Facebook is only something that has existed for under a year. As time goes on, the algorithm that targets the advertising is likely to become more advanced and more effective at doing this in a highly targeted way.

Mobile social media: conclusions

As well as needing to consider all of the usual complexities of social media when planning our mobile activities, we have some additional things to take into account. We still need to consider appropriate use of channels, focus on content and engagement and find effective measurement strategies. Most importantly with mobile social media, we need to consider the overall user experience and be very much focussed on trust.

User experience is all down to making sure we have thought through and tested how the user will actually experience our social media content and how they can engage with us. Although time consuming and fragmented, due to the number of possible devices and scenarios involved, it is a very practical and reasonably straight-forward issue.

Trust on the other hand is far more subjective but of huge importance. Mobile devices can act as magnifiers for missteps we make as marketers. By interrupting, being irrelevant or making incorrect assumptions, we will actually inconvenience our target audience when they are most likely to find this annoying. This may be by giving them much more irrelevant content to scroll past or bombarding them with the same message again and again.

As with all social media, mobile social can be a double-edged sword: it gives us great opportunity but also carries risks. This means that now more than ever, mobile social media requires well-thought-out and considered plans that focus on providing value to the user.

CASE STUDY   FAW-Benteng and Tencent

Industry

Automotive

Location

China

Marketing objectives

Improve awareness and brand affinity to drive long-term car sales

Their solution

A multi-channel social media campaign to engage with Chinese consumers via an emotive family-focussed video. The video communicated the concerns and challenges of many Chinese commuters working far away from home. The 'Bring Love Home' campaign associated the automotive brand with being a positive part of consumers' lives and helping them spend more time with their family. This was achieved using a core video on Tencent Video, editorial content on QQ.com and encouraging the sharing of a Bring Love Home badge on QQ Instant Messenger (the market-leading chat platform).

Their results

- drove 'Bring Love Home' into a top 10 search term during the campaign;

- 8 million video views;

- 18 million tweets and comments;

- 99 per cent positive sentiment in user-generated content;

- 20 per cent increase in brand awareness in target market.

What's good about it

The target audiences for FAW-Benteng and the profile of Tencent social media platform users were well aligned. The campaign was centred around emotive video content that stimulated conversation and this was carried across the mobile social media user journey. This led to increased brand awareness and brand affinity via highly positive social engagement.

Mobile search

Mobile search is growing phenomenally, with both Google and Baidu reporting over 1,000 per cent growth in search on mobile devices in the past three years (SearchEngineLand, 2013). With more and more users relying on mobile searches, and evidence showing that around 73 per cent of mobile searches end in an action (Researchscape, 2013), mobile search is an essential part of any mobile strategy.

Defining mobile search

We would normally divide search into two key areas: natural or organic search, the area of the search results decided upon by the search engines; and paid search, the set of results that we can pay to be visible in. Search engine optimization (SEO) is the process of achieving search rankings within the natural/organic results. Pay-per-click (PPC) refers to the paid search element of search results. We'll explore both in this chapter.

SEM: my least favourite three letter acronym

As you have probably already worked out, we love three letter acronyms in digital marketing. Of all these acronyms, SEM is my least favourite. It stands for 'search engine marketing', and technically (I'll happily argue till I'm blue in the face over this) speaking, it means both sides of search marketing, that is both SEO and PPC. However, it is often used to describe the paid side of search, PPC. Because of this ambiguity, I won't be using it again in this book!

In reality, we could place PPC within the advertising section of this book, because that's exactly what it is: a form of paid advertising. However, the term 'online advertising' is most often used to refer to banner and video ads, so for the sake of consistency with this definition, we'll discuss PPC within this section of the book.

Desktop vs mobile results

The major search engines, and particularly Google, will try to give a mobile-optimized search experience. This means you will be given different search results depending on the device you search on. This optimization, which may show data such as local results on a map, combined with the mobile's limited screen space, means that it is even more important that your search result comes as near to the top as possible.

The screenshot in Figure 12.1 shows the kind of results you will see when searching for something that includes a location-specific term. The results shown are a mix of paid search (at the very top of the page), followed by one organic search result (in this case TripAdvisor) and then a series of results shown on a map. This makes a lot of sense from a user-experience point of view, but makes things even more challenging when optimizing for desktop search, due to the limited amount of space given to organic search results (although the map results are actually a form of organic search results). This means that maximizing our chances of showing in the map results is essential.

Most search engines offer some form of local business registration, when your business has some form of physical presence. Generally, registering your business within the mapping element of a search engine, such as Baidu, Bing or Google Maps, will help these results. Google has merged its local business listings service into Google+, its own social network, and we will discuss this in more detail later.

The screen shot in Figure 12.2 shows customized search results based on the physical location of the user searching. I live in Brighton in the UK, so my results have been optimized to try and show me local results, because Google has decided the term I am searching for

FIGURE 12.1 Mobile search results: location-specific term (www.google.com)

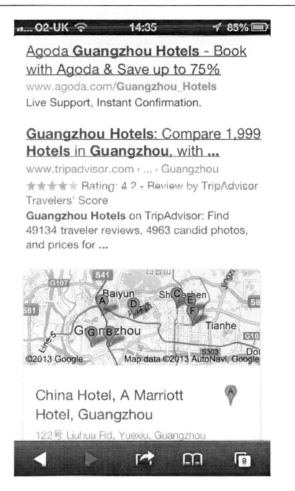

has location-based properties. For this reason, when you are doing your keyword research (a topic we will discuss in more depth shortly) it is important to try your search terms out on a mobile device to see the kind of results you are getting. Again, in this case, making sure I am listed in the map results is important, and paid search is also very visible and is actually shown above the results on this screenshot.

We are able to target PPC advertising specifically at mobile devices, and to give particular functionality to our ads that can help the mobile experience, such as 'click-to-call' buttons. We'll explore the PPC options in more depth shortly, but first we are going to explore how we get to the top of the organic search results.

FIGURE 12.2   Mobile search: results based on user location
(www.google.com)

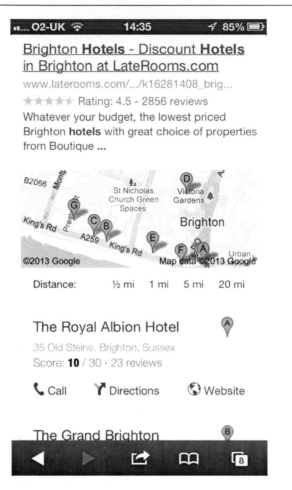

The PPC/SEO relationship

There has always been discussion and rumour around how much your SEO
results are boosted by spending money on PPC campaigns. The answer, for
the vast majority of search engines, is that there is no direct correlation
whatsoever. I have had clients spending millions of pounds every month,
and there was no direct impact on their natural search rankings. This rule,
however, doesn't follow for Baidu, the largest search engine in China.
Fundamentally, the more you are spending with Baidu, the better your natural
search visibility tends to be. It's a nice easy way to get search rankings, but
probably not the best way to give the user the most relevant search results.

Search engine optimization (SEO)

SEO is all about getting to the top of the search engine results in the organic results. Thankfully the core rules of SEO are consistent across both mobile and desktop searches, and we'll explore these core concepts here. We'll also look at the differences between mobile and desktop search and what you can do to make sure you are maximizing your visibility and therefore your traffic and visitors.

It all starts with spiders

Spiders are bits of software that read your pages and send the content back to the search engines. If they can't read your site, you won't get rankings.

The search engine spiders (also known as 'bots' or 'robots') visit your website, follow the links on your pages and send your content back to the search engine so it can be assessed and ranked. This data is known as the search engine's index. Generally, the more often you update your content and the more important your website is seen as being (we'll cover this 'importance' when we look at link building), the more often the spiders will come back to look at your content.

There are certain practices that can stop the spiders from reading your content in the first place, and clearly, if your website can't be read, you won't get ranked. A good example of this is building your entire site in Flash. Flash is a proprietary technology from Adobe that allows you to build animated and interactive web content. Google and the other search engines find it difficult, or choose not to read the content inside Flash. This basically means the search engine sees the 'box' that contains the content, rather than the content itself. You should also remember that Flash will not work on an iOS device, so it is to be avoided on mobile sites.

Google and some of the other search engine spiders will attempt to visit your site and act as a mobile device to look for a mobile-optimized experience (Google, 2013). Sites that are offering an improved mobile experience are then given a boost within the search rankings. This evidence is somewhat subjective, however, as the spiders can detect a difference between desktop and mobile sites, but cannot determine whether it is an optimal experience.

Google operators

If you want to check that Google is visiting your website and when the spiders last visited, you can use the following technique, known as a Google operator. Go to Google as normal, but instead of searching for a word or phrase, type the following into the search box: cache: **www.yourwebsite.com**.

This will bring back a copy of your website and some details that tell you when Google last visited your site. If this returns nothing it may mean that Google isn't visiting your website.

Google Webmaster Tools

For some real insight into how Google's spiders are accessing your pages and any problems they may be having, you need to install Google Webmaster Tools. You can find Google Webmaster Tools here: **http://www.google.com/webmasters/tools/**.

You'll need a Google account to set things up (you can set one up in a couple of minutes) and you'll then need to prove that you own the website you want to get some details on. Google provides step-by-step instructions, but you will need to be able either to edit your web pages code or to create a new page with a specific name (as this demonstrates to Google that you control the website).

Once installed, Google Webmaster Tools do the following:

- **Get Google's view of your site and diagnose problems** – you can see how Google crawls and indexes your site and learn about specific problems they're having accessing it. Probably the most important feature in regard to what we've been talking about.

- **Discover your links and query traffic** – you can view and download data about internal and external links to your site with the link-reporting tools. Find out which Google search words/phrases drive traffic to your site, and see exactly how users arrive there.

- **Share information about your site** – this allows you to tell Google about your pages with Sitemaps: which pages are the most important to you and how often they change.

It also has some features that allow you to see how fast your pages load in comparison to other sites. This is important as it is one of the factors that Google considers when deciding your rankings.

Keyword research for SEO

Keyword research is all about understanding how your potential audience searches so you know what search phrases you need to rank for. Once we've done this we need to look at getting the words onto our pages, and we'll cover this when we discuss on-page optimization.

It's too easy to make assumptions about what words and phrases our potential audience is searching for based on our own opinions (or possibly the opinions of our search agency). We need to back this up with real facts, and happily, there are plenty of free tools that allow us to do just this.

Keyword challenges

Some of the everyday challenges you'll face in keyword research are best demonstrated by giving an example. When I ran a search agency we had a large recruitment client whose basic brief was: we want to be number 1 for the word 'jobs'. What they were basically asking for was to be ranked first out of about 3,600,000,000 (just search for a phrase in Google and you'll see, just above your search results, the approximate number of pages that Google has in its index containing the searched phrase). We did it (and they are still in the top five) but was this worth the effort and cost?

Generic search terms

Achieving number 1 positions for broad and generic search terms like this just won't be achievable for most of us (at least in the short term). We won't have the resources (financial or time) to achieve this. In reality we'd also be wasting a lot of time. Who searches for the word 'jobs'? It's most likely to be someone that's assessing the marketplace of recruitment websites. They're at the browsing stage of the online journey and are probably pretty unlikely to be applying for a job on this first visit. In reality if we start by saying, 'I want to be number 1 for "digital marketing jobs London"', we start to target people nearer the point of conversion (when they are actually going to do something) and we're going to be competing against a lot fewer people (588,000 in this particular case, which is a lot better than billions!).

So why would a large organization like the recruitment website I mentioned go for such a generic search term? There are a few reasons outlined below:

- **Ignorance** – they may not know very much about SEO.

- **Long term** – it's valid to approach more generic terms in the long term. It's achievable if you're willing to keep working at it and it can make up part of a mixed keyword strategy (this is when you target lots of phrases with lots of combinations of phrases on a topic).

- **Volume** – if you sell online advertising you may be more interested in volume than quality. This is because online ads are generally sold CPM (cost per mille or, basically, cost per thousand views). So, advertisers are charged each time a page is loaded, without taking into account the type of user loading the page.

Long-tail search

According to SearchEngineWatch, over 50 per cent of searches are done with three or more word phrases. The more specific the phrase we search on, the clearer we are on what we are looking for and the more likely a search is to lead to an action. Some form of action, like a purchase, download, application etc is what we generally want to achieve as marketers, so these longer, or 'long-tail', phrases are what we should often focus on. The phrase 'long-tail' comes from the idea that there is a wide selection of search phrases made up of multiple words that will not drive huge volume (although using multiple long-tail phrases can drive lots of traffic), but are more likely to drive conversion.

Keyword variations

We also need to understand exactly how people search and the order and variations of words that they use. Google wants to match exactly what you've searched for, so the difference between 'jobs Manchester' and 'Manchester jobs' is important. Which variation do most people search on? Luckily Google provides tools that can tell us exactly this, and the two main tools are discussed below.

Keyword tool

The Keyword tool is great for finding the actual number (or at least a fairly accurate estimate) of searches for a particular term, which can be looked at globally or country by country. This tool also shows suggested variations of the search term and how many searches these get per month, so it's a fantastic tool for building a list of words for which we want to optimize our pages. Always look at the volume of searches vs how competitive the search term is going to be. The easiest way to do this is just to search the term and see how many results come back in Google: the higher the number, generally the more competition there will be.

One of most important things about the Keyword tool from a mobile perspective is that it allows you to separate mobile and desktop searches, so you can see the different ways in which users are searching (see Figure 12.3).

FIGURE 12.3   Selecting mobile and/or desktop searches in the keyword tool (http://adwords.google.co.uk/o/Targeting/Explorer)

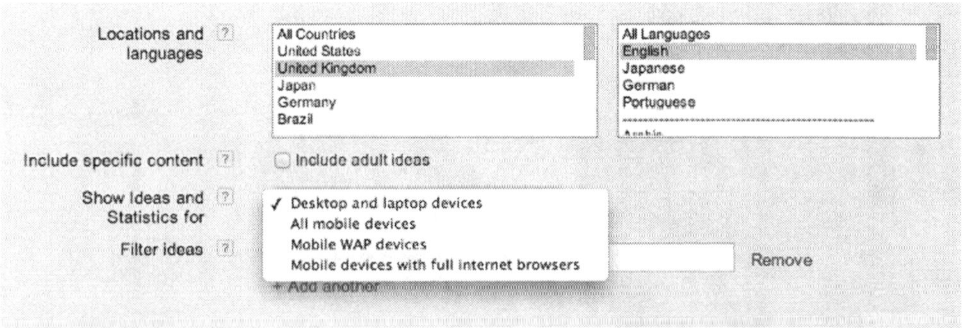

FIGURE 12.4 Keyword variations and volumes of searches on mobile devices (http://adwords.google.co.uk/o/Targeting/Explorer)

Keyword	Competition	Global Monthly Searches ?	Local Monthly Searches ?
mobile marketing ▾	High	22,200	1,600

Save all **Keyword ideas (100)**   1 – 50 of 100 ▶

Keyword	Competition	Global Monthly Searches ?	Local Monthly Searches ?
mobile marketing magazine ▾	High	140	110
mobile marketing association ▾	High	260	22
mobile marketing agency ▾	High	110	28
mobile marketing companies ▾	High	320	16
mobile marketing awards ▾	Medium	22	12
mobile marketing uk ▾	High	46	36
mobile marketing strategies ▾	High	210	16
best mobile on the market ▾	High	3,600	720
mobile phone marketing ▾	High	590	58
mobile marketing news ▾	High	58	< 10
mobile text marketing ▾	High	140	12
mobile apps market ▾	Medium	3,600	320

The screenshot in Figure 12.4 shows the results when looking at the phrase 'mobile marketing' searched for on mobile devices. We are given the number of searches per month globally, locally (in the country we have set it to) and a selection of other related search terms.

Google Trends: http://www.google.com/trends

Google Trends can tell us quite a lot about how people search, but its key capability is in showing trends over time and comparing search terms. Enter a search term and it will show you the trend over time of people searching for that term. It doesn't show an actual number of searches, but rather the trend (the Keyword tool tells us actual numbers which we'll look at in a moment). We can also enter multiple terms and see how they compare. Its other key capability is to show geographical interest in a term by country, which can then be drilled down to by region and city. Always remember that when two countries are compared, it is showing where somebody is more likely to be searching, not necessarily that there is actually a larger volume of searches in that country. Finally, we get a selection of other words that have been searched on in relation to this term, which are the most popular, and which have grown most in the past year.

This screenshot in Figure 12.5 shows the comparison of the search terms 'blackberry', 'nokia' and 'iphone' in the UK market. We can see a direct correlation between the market for these brands and the volume of searches for them. Also remember that bad news stories, such as the 'Blackberry blackout', when the Blackberry network stopped working for a number of days, will also cause a peak in searches.

SEO, local search and Google+

We've already seen the importance of local search, and how maps can dominate the mobile search results for some types of searches. For this reason we need to maximize our opportunities of getting listed on this map-based result. Bing, Yahoo, Baidu, Yandex and Google all allow you to list your location on a map via their mapping services. The more detail you can add to these map-based listings the better, and generally by connecting these listings to your website (which all of these search engines allow you to do), you stand a better chance of showing up in the map results in a mobile search.

FIGURE 12.5   Google Trends: comparing search terms
(www.google.com/trends)

Google has taken a different approach, and has merged its local business results into its Google+ platform. Google+ is essentially a social network that offers much of the functionality of sites like Facebook and LinkedIn. However, at this stage it's worth thinking of Google+ as a social 'layer' on top of search, that gives Google the ability to more precisely match your search requirements to the results that you are given. There are some elements of Google+ that are already changing desktop search results and it's fairly logical that this will evolve into mobile search as well, but what is clear is that a Google+ local business listing can help you appear in the map results on both mobile and desktop devices.

FIGURE 12.6   Google+: a local business result (http://plus.google.com)

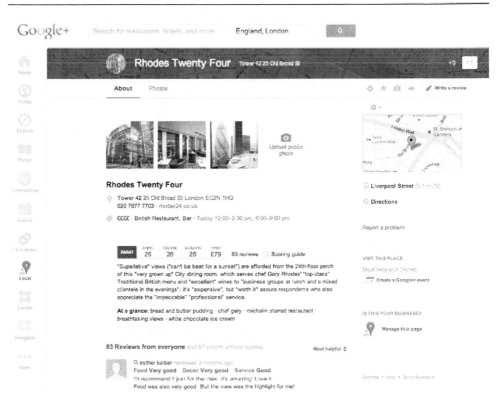

The screenshot in Figure 12.6 shows that local business listings, along with map results and reviews, have been automatically turned into Google+ pages. You can also see that on the right hand side of the screen you can 'manage this page' by taking ownership, and this allows you to expand and enhance your listings.

On-page optimization

So far we have explored the topics of search engine spiders and keyword research. This means we've made sure the search spiders can access our web pages and we've identified the words that we want to achieve rankings for. The next stage is to actually get these words onto our pages. On-page optimization is all about getting the right words on the page, in the right place. We've identified the right words during the keyword research phase, and now we need to put them in the right places. This is actually a fairly straightforward process and is just a matter of looking at the core elements of a page and factoring our words and phrases in.

Users first, then search engines

What we are trying to do is help the search engines understand the content on our web pages. However, we don't want to do this at the expense of the user journey. What I mean is that if we over-optimize our content it will actually make our copy hard to read. You can drive all the traffic in the world, but if everybody leaves when they start trying to read your content, you've wasted your time. Focus on getting things right for the user first and then we'll adapt things as appropriate for the search engines.

I've listed below the key areas of the page that are of most importance and then we'll look at each of these elements in more detail:

- page title;
- web page names;
- headings;
- copy;
- alt text;
- link text;
- file names.

Each of these different parts of your web pages gives us the opportunity to show the search engines what the pages are all about. So let's take a look at them in a little more detail (see Figure 12.7).

Page title

The page title is still the most important thing on the page as it is generally given the greatest weighting by the search engines and it is actually what shows up in many search engines (including Google) as the main title in the search engine results pages (SERP).

FIGURE 12.7 Search engine optimization: key elements of the page (www.targetinternet.com)

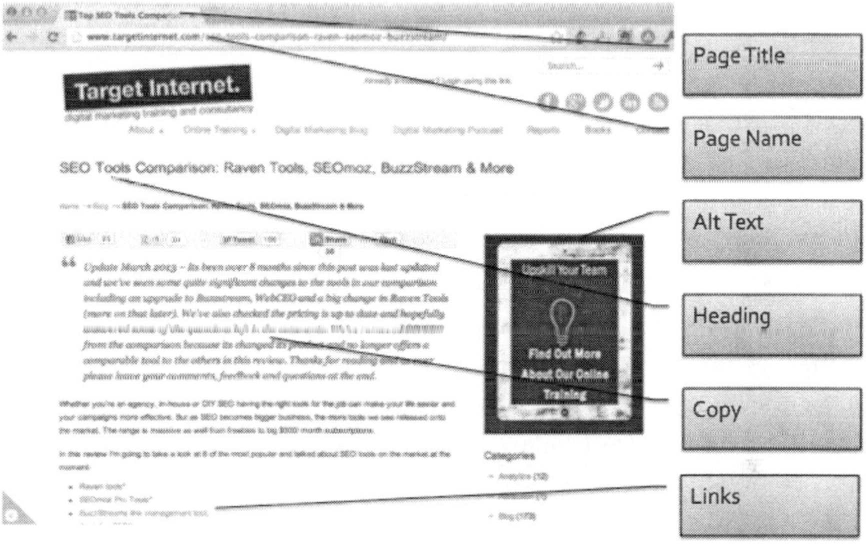
Target Internet.
SEO Tools Comparison: Raven Tools, SEOmoz, BuzzStream & More
Page Title
Page Name
Alt Text
Heading
Copy
Links

FIGURE 12.8 Page title: main line of the Google search result

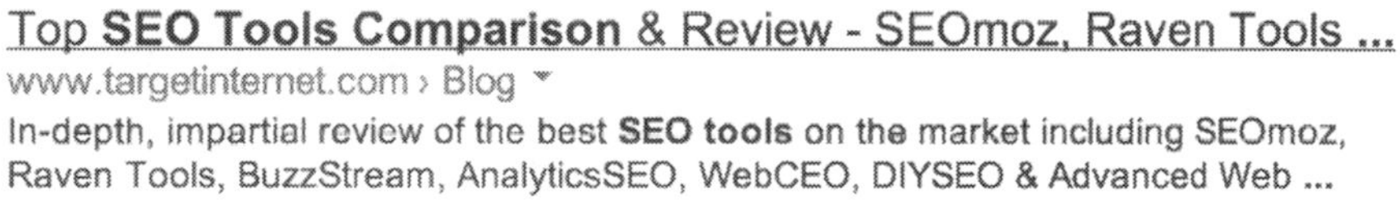
Top SEO Tools Comparison & Review - SEOmoz, Raven Tools ...
www.targetinternet.com › Blog
In-depth, impartial review of the best SEO tools on the market including SEOmoz, Raven Tools, BuzzStream, AnalyticsSEO, WebCEO, DIYSEO & Advanced Web ...

The page title (see Figure 12.8) is actually something that shows up in the top bar or tab of your browser window, and is something that most users don't even notice when using your web pages. It's actually something that is initially written by your web developer or content management system, and is one of the most commonly missed and most effective elements of SEO. Huge numbers of website page titles are blank or say things like 'home'. In other cases people repeat the same page title again and again or use their company name. If I am looking for your company name that's fine, but what about when I am searching for what you do? A good page title factors in a range of phrases that a user may search for.

So for example 'online digital marketing training from Target Internet' is a much better page title than 'Target Internet' as it says what my site actually offers and includes the words and phrases that a user might actually search for.

Headings

The headings and sub-headings throughout your pages help the search engines to understand the key themes of these pages. Again, these should factor in the most important words and phrases that a user may be searching for and that you have identified during your keyword research.

The spiders are actually reading the code of your pages rather than looking at the code as we do. The headings in your copy are represented as 'H' tags. These are parts of the HTML code that go to build your pages, and you actually have up to six different tiers or heading tags. The H1 tag is your main heading, the H2 tag is for sub-headings and so on all the way through to H6. In reality we most often don't get past using H1s and H2s, which is absolutely fine from an SEO perspective. It's important to understand though that you should only ever have one H1 but you can have multiple H2s. The logic behind having only one H1 is so that you are clearly indicating the core theme of your page. Multiple H1s would water down this core theme and make it harder for the search engines to understand the real focus of your page. This is a common mistake and should be avoided.

Bear in mind that the actual part of your page that is used as an H1, H2 etc will be decided by either the person who originally coded your page or the content management system (CMS) that you are using. For this reason it may be necessary to have the code of your pages modified to use the appropriate part of the page as heading tags. Thankfully in systems such as Wordpress this is all taken care of for you in a very sensible way.

Web page names

Your website address and the actual names of the pages that you create will again act as indicators for the search engines as to what your content is about. This doesn't mean your actual website name must include your keywords, but it does mean that you should name your pages appropriately. For example, my website doesn't have to be called **www.mobilemarketing.com** if that is the topic of the content (although in an ideal world it would be), but if I create a page on this topic I should name it **www.mywebsite.com/mobile-marketing**. This is because the search engines are realistic in realizing that many of our websites' addresses are actually our company names and so on. Again, this may be impacted by your original developer or CMS, and systems like Wordpress allow you to control this easily.

Copy

The main copy on your pages should include your targeted key phrases, ideally in the first paragraph. However, you certainly don't need to keep repeating the words again and again. In fact, if you do keep repeating the words, not only can you make the copy hard to read, it could actually be interpreted as negative by the search engines (see the box below on 'black hat SEO').

Black hat vs white hat SEO

What we are talking about is ethical, or so called 'white hat', SEO. This means we are trying to help the search engines to understand our content. There is also something called 'black hat' SEO that is all about trying to manipulate the search engines. If you get caught using black hat techniques you can get completely removed from some search engine results, and Google is particularly effective at detecting these techniques.

The main rule is that the website content should be there for the user and not the search engines and that what the user is shown is what the spiders should also see. If you want to understand more about what Google expects and considers to be best practice, you can take a look at their webmaster guidelines: **http://www.google.com/webmasters/**.

Link text

The actual words that we choose to create the link from on our web pages help the search engine understand the relevance of the page we are linking to (it also helps set the context of the page we are linking from to some extent). These actual words we are using to link are referred to as 'anchor text', and it's an important indicator for the search engines. For this reason we shouldn't use such phrases as 'click here' or 'read more' as these are essentially meaningless to the search engines. These types of phrase also make it harder for a user scanning your page to quickly identify its core themes.

File names

Although only a small factor, the names of the files that make up your pages have some impact on the search engines' understanding of your web pages. So you should name your images, video files etc appropriately to describe their content and where possible factor in your key words and phrases.

Alt text

Alt text is text that describes an image and is put in place by a developer or using a CMS. The alt text is there for accessibility reasons primarily, but also has an impact on SEO. Accessibility is all about making your website usable by people who need to use it in a different way for some reason. For example, if I am a blind user, in order to use the web I will use something called a screen-reader. A screen-reader is a piece of software that reads out web pages in a simulated voice. When this reader gets to an image, it can't understand that image so it reads out the alt text instead. The search engines have a similar problem and don't understand images either. For this reason they then read the alt text to better understand the image.

As I have said, the alt text is actually for accessibility and SEO should be a secondary consideration. However, if you can factor in your keywords and phrases into these descriptions, it does help with your overall SEO efforts. You should also be aware that effective use of alt tags is very important and is actually a legal requirement within the European Union under the Disability Discrimination Act. Wherever you are based, however, alt tags are important to help people access your website, and they have an impact on SEO.

On-page optimization in perspective

Once you've been through the process of identifying your most important words and phrases, and you have made sure they have been put into your pages in the appropriate places, you have done the fundamentals of on-page optimization. The search engines get smarter and smarter about understanding how different topics and themes are inter-connected, and Google in particular is getting very good at understanding the context as well as the words of a particular piece of content. For this reason, you shouldn't obsess over on-page optimization too much, but rather focus on providing value through your content. That leads us into the extremely important next step in SEO.

On-page optimization and responsive sites

Always remember that whatever elements of the page display on a responsive site will have a fundamental impact on your on-page optimization of that page. There is increasing evidence that the search engines are looking at how our devices display on different devices and are judging the content accordingly. Each of the various page elements is still important, but we need to look at how they differ on each device.

Link building

If on-page optimization is telling the search engines what your content is about, link building is telling the search engines the authority of that content. A link to your content from somewhere else is basically seen as a vote of confidence. People only link to content they find useful or interesting, and therefore links are essential to your search optimization efforts.

Neither on-page optimization nor link building can work in isolation, as both are needed to understand the topic and authority of your site and its content. Driving more links to increase your authority is all about creating engaging and interesting content, and this is one of the reasons why 'content marketing' has become such an important approach in recent years. If our websites just say how great we are or how great our product is, there is little reason for anyone to link to us. However, if we provide value via our content, we are encouraging links, building value and potentially driving engagement.

For example, my own website's primary commercial aim is to drive enquiries for an e-learning product, but the majority of the site's content is actually all about giving free digital marketing advice. This free advice takes the form of blog posts, podcasts and reports. All of this content drives links from other websites where people find this content useful or interesting, and in turn drives my site up the search rankings.

Link building and mobile sites

In most cases many links you get from other sites won't actually link to your mobile site. This will be particularly true if you are using some form of responsive site, as there may be no mobile-specific URL and the site only becomes a mobile site when the browsing device is detected. Don't worry about this at all. Focus on creating content that drives links; this will then be interpreted by the search engines in the appropriate way.

Social signals

As well as looking at the number of links to our content we have from other sites, the search engines are increasingly concerned with what we call 'social signals'. These social signals are the conversations that are happening in social media about your site and content. This is not to say that you can tweet about your own site a thousand times, and you'll suddenly leap to the top of the search rankings! In Chapter 11 we looked at the social scoring service Klout that attempts to score the social influence of a particular user or social media account. In reality the major search engines have an internal process that works in a similar way, and they are trying to access both the quantity and quality of social signals that are being created about your content.

This increasingly means that using social media to get users discussing, engaging with and sharing your content is highly important. Sharing your latest content with the appropriate social platforms can not only create social signals but also encourage further links to your content.

Measuring link authority

There are a number of tools and methods for measuring how effective our link building strategies are and how authoritative our sites are seen as being. All of these are actually looking at two key things: the quality and quantity of links and social signals to our content.

Search engine algorithms

Much of what SEO agencies concern themselves with is understanding the algorithms the search engines use to decide how your content is ranked in the search results. In my opinion this is increasingly a waste of time. The smarter the search engines get, the more complex their algorithms become and the more of a nonsense it becomes trying to decode this set of rules. I was actually told by somebody at Google that in reality, even within Google, there would only be a handful of people who know and understand the complete set of rules because it is such a complicated and huge thing. Rather than focussing on trying to outwit the engineers at Google (good luck with that!), we should focus on the fundamental issue of creating useful and engaging content.

Open Site Explorer

The first of the tools we'll look at is the excellent Open Site Explorer tool from moz.com (see Figure 12.9). Moz.com offers a huge range of SEO tools as part of its paid monthly subscription. You can also access Open Site Explorer in a limited way for free. It doesn't give you all of the features, results are limited and you can only use it three times in any one day, but it's still fantastically useful.

When you enter a website or particular web page into the tool it gives you a range of information about the quantity and quality of links to that page. You are given a score out of one hundred for the authority of your domain as well as any particular page you are looking at. It's a great way of benchmarking yourself, and you can do the same for your competitors. The paid version will also show some data on social signals from a limited number of social sites.

FIGURE 12.9 Open Site Explorer from moz.com (www.opensiteexplorer.org)

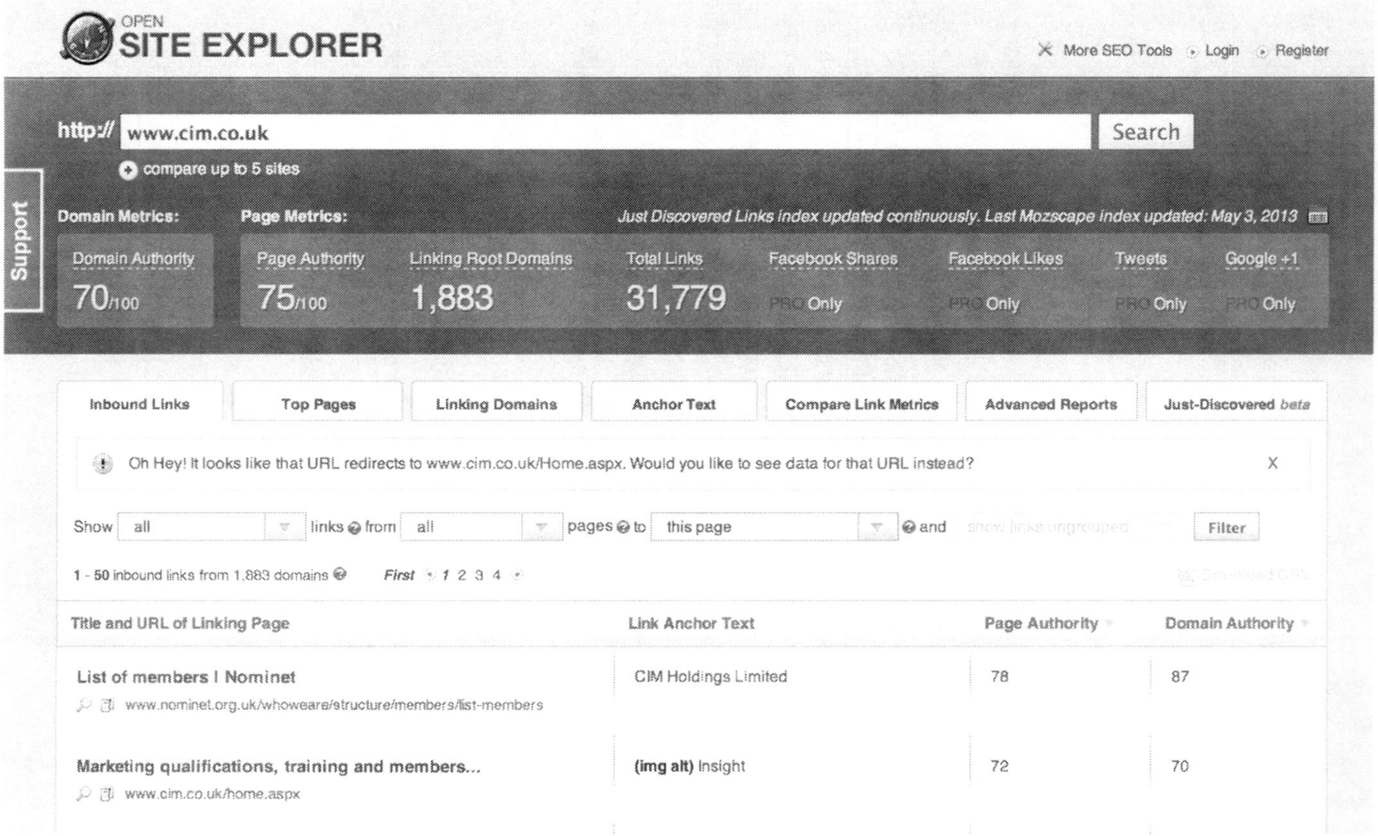

Google PageRank

Google's PageRank is a score between 0 and 10 given to every web page that Google looks at. This score is based on the quantity and quality of links to your content. The quality of the links is in turn based on their page rank. Therefore, links from websites with a high page rank help boost your page rank. PageRank makes up part of the Google algorithm and is an indicator of how much trust or authority Google sees your site and content as having. There is some discussion about how much weighting PageRank is actually given, but we don't need to concern ourselves with that too much at this stage.

There are a number of ways to find the PageRank score for your particular site or page. The first and probably easiest way in the long term is to install a plug-in for your browser. I use the Google Chrome browser, and a simple Google search of 'Chrome PageRank plug-in' returns me a number of options. Once installed, for every page I visit I can see its score out of ten in the top right corner of my browser. Figure 12.10 shows a PageRank plug-in in action in Google Chrome.

Be aware that the PageRank score that we see is always out of date and is only updated a few times a year. It's still a good long-term indicator though. PageRank 7 websites tend to beat PageRank 3 websites in the search rankings every time. It's a fairly blunt measure, but it's an easy one to monitor and should be seen as part of your SEO measurement, not the be-all-and-end-all of SEO measurement.

If you're interested in search engines other than Google, like Yandex or Baidu, they too have their own scoring mechanisms. (Yandex's scoring mechanism is called Thematic Citation Index (TIC): **http://help.yandex.com/webmaster/?id=1125342**). The reality is that they all look at the quality and quantity of links pointing to your content. Although they all calculate the 'quality' differently, the same core rules apply.

FIGURE 12.10 Google Chrome and PageRank plug-in (http://chrome.google.com/webstore/)

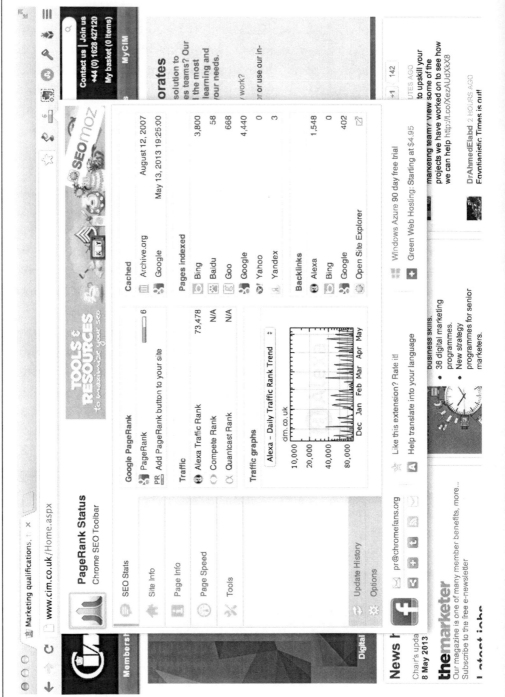

Mobile SEO: conclusions

So, just like SEO in general, we can sum up mobile SEO into some fairly straightforward key steps:

- spiders – make sure that your content is visible to the search engines;

- keyword research – understand what your target audience is searching for and build a list of words and phrases that you would like to rank for;

- on-page optimization – get these words on your page in the right places;

- link building – build a content-based strategy to encourage links to and discussions around your content;

- benchmarking – measure and improve your SEO efforts.

The additional steps you need to consider specifically for mobile SEO are:

- mapping and location-based listings – make sure you are listed and have fully registered your site with any location-based services including mapping sites and things like Google+ local business pages.

- mobile site auditing – make sure your mobile site on-page elements are in line with the key themes of your content.

Paid search

Pay-per-click (PPC) is the other side of search, and due to the limitations of screen space in mobile search, it is even more visible and dominates more of available screen space than within desktop search. We'll look at the pros and cons of PPC in detail, but its key advantage is our ability to control and target it precisely.

If you receive a promise of a number 1 search ranking from an agency or freelancer, one of two things is happening. They are either talking about PPC, or they are lying. Nobody can guarantee you number 1 rankings in Google, even somebody who has done it a thousand times before, because only Google control it.

Within the major PPC systems we are able to target particular ads at mobile users. This means we control what ads are seen on mobile devices and can change the content shown in these ads accordingly. Want to promote an app? Add a link that allows you to click straight to a map? How about a link to dial a number? All possible with mobile PPC and all things that make it increasingly likely that we can drive action from these ads (see Figure 12.11).

Another advantage of PPC is speed. We can be number 1 in the search rankings almost immediately if we are willing to pay for it. Organic search can take months to achieve rankings for competitive terms, and even then it's not guaranteed. Also, don't mistake organic search for being free. Although you don't pay for every click, you are going to spend time and effort creating content and so on.

PPC is an auction-based system. The more you are willing to pay per click, the more visibility your ad will generally get. This also means that the more competitive your industry and the words you choose to target both are, the more expensive it can become. More on this later.

FIGURE 12.11   Mobile paid search in Google (www.google.co.uk)

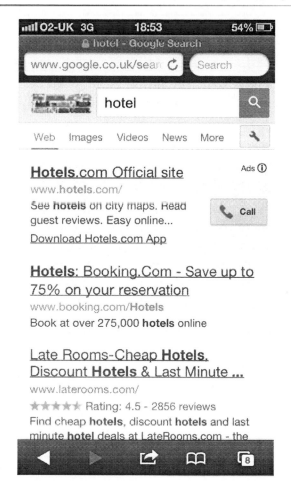

PPC fundamentals

We'll take a look at each of the key steps involved in planning and implementing a successful mobile PPC campaign shown in the list below:

- keyword research;
- create ad copy;
- select additional ad features;
- set targeting criteria;
- set budgets and bids.

PPC keyword research

There will certainly be commonality between the keyword research you do for your SEO campaigns and your PPC campaigns, and you will use many of the same tools. However, one fundamental to understand about PPC, is the more precise your selection of words, and the better matched these are to your ad copy and landing pages, the more successful your campaign will be.

The words you select for your PPC campaigns will trigger your ads. You could select a generic search term to trigger your ad so that you get lots of traffic. This is a very good way to spend lots of money and get few results. You could also use lots of different search terms to trigger the same generic ad. Again, a good way to waste your budget. Generally, a very specific key phrase that triggers a specific ad which sends the searcher to a very specific and relevant landing page will get the most from your budget.

A really important consideration when looking at mobile paid search is that of location-based search terms. A location-based search term is most likely to end in action on a mobile device (SearchEngineLand, 2013), so these terms can be highly valuable. We'll talk more about location-based targeting later.

Create ad copy

Fundamentally a PPC ad is made up of a number of lines of text (it may also include an image on platforms such as Facebook) and a link (or a number of links) through to your site. This copy is what grabs the searcher's attention and attracts the click-through to your site. We won't go into copywriting techniques here as much has been written on the topic already, but what we must think about in regard to writing our ads for mobile users is context. When I search on a mobile device, I am more likely to be at the point of conversion (actually carrying out an action) than when I search on a desktop (Researchscape, 2013). For this reason, the wording of my ads needs to reflect this context.

Bear in mind you can create multiple versions of your ad copy and most PPC systems will automatically rotate these ads and tell you which ad is attracting the most clicks and/or conversions on your site.

Google moves to a context focus

A very important move, that very closely reflects many of the issues we have discussed in this book, is Google moving its PPC system (AdWords) to a context-based model. What this means is that we aren't just doing one ad for mobile and one for mobile.

What we are actually doing is setting up a single campaign that has a number of different options based on the context of your search. That will include what device you are searching on, the time of day and your location. Based on this context I can use different ad options and set my bids accordingly. For a great example of this in action, let's take a look at an example from Google:

> *Sally's Flower Shop has a physical shop on Main Street and a website where customers can order online.*
>
> Within a single campaign, Sally can customize ad headlines, text and landing pages so that people using smartphones see ads that take them to her mobile site, while people using computers and tablets see relevant links on her desktop website. And when her shop is open, Sally has ads that show links to a shop locator as well as her business phone number for smartphone users. When her shop closes at 5 pm, she sets her ads to only show links to her website where customers can place their orders. With Enhanced Campaigns, Sally is able to schedule when and on which devices she would like these ad extensions to appear.

For more on Enhanced Campaigns (I'm guessing the name has limited lifetime, as all campaigns are being moved to this format!) take a look at the guide from Google: **http://www.google.co.uk/adwords/enhancedcampaigns**. A screenshot of the Enhanced Campaign in Figure 12.12 shows its focus on context-based ad campaigns.

Additional ad features

Google and Baidu offer a number of additional ad options, some of them specific to mobile searches and others that are available for all ads. A mobile-specific example is a 'click-to-call' button, allowing users

FIGURE 12.12   Google's Enhanced Campaign (www.google.com/adwords/enhancedcampaigns)

to call your telephone number directly from your ad. In Google, for example, you can include links to multiple pages of your website if your ad is in one of the top positions. Being in these top positions, however, will depend on your bid (how much you are willing to pay for a click). You can also add links to maps of your location to your ads.

These additional ad features serve two purposes. The first is clearly to encourage users to take an action in response to your ads. Secondly, they can make your ad more likely to be noticed as they differentiate your ad visually, and generally add to the overall size of the ad. We have mentioned several times that you are more likely to carry out some sort of immediate action after a mobile search than after a desktop search, and these additional call-to-action buttons can increase this likelihood further. Both Google and SearchEngine-Land have reported that over one third of location-based searches that result in a call have that call made on a mobile device (Search-EngineLand, 2013).

Set targeting criteria

The targeting criteria you set for your ads is particularly important for mobile ads. You can target by the type of device somebody is searching on (split between desktop, smartphone and tablet) as well as target by location-based criteria. Location-based targeting is split into three key areas in Google, and most other systems follow similar principles (although accuracy can be poor in Baidu in particular). These location-based criteria are:

- Targeting by physical location that the search is made in (eg searching for 'hotels' while in New York).

- Targeting by what people are searching for (eg searching for 'hotels in New York').

- Targeting by intent – this is based on various factors that Google consider, such as previous searches (eg searching for 'hotels' after having searched 'trip to New York' and 'best deals flights New York').

Set budgets and bids

As well as setting your daily budget (the maximum you are willing to spend each day) you can set your maximum cost-per-click (CPC). CPC is the main factor that decides where your ad shows up on the page. Because PPC systems generally work on an auction basis, the more you are willing to pay per click, the higher up the page your ad appears and the more visibility it has. That visibility should lead to clicks, assuming your ad content is appealing to the searcher. You shouldn't always assume, however, that it's always better to be in the top positions on the page. You may find that being further down the page means you are paying less per click and getting clicks more slowly, but you get better value overall from your budget. This is one of the many reasons that, to get the maximum value from your budget, you need to test and adjust your campaigns on an ongoing basis.

CPC can be set at a number of different levels. You can apply a single maximum CPC to group of ads or just for a particular key phrase. Many systems, including Google, have an automatic bidding option that will try and maximize the number of clicks you receive for your budget. Just remember though that the maximum volume of traffic doesn't necessarily mean the maximum amount of conversions on your site.

FIGURE 12.13   Google AdWords: adjusting bids according to device (www.google.com/adwords)

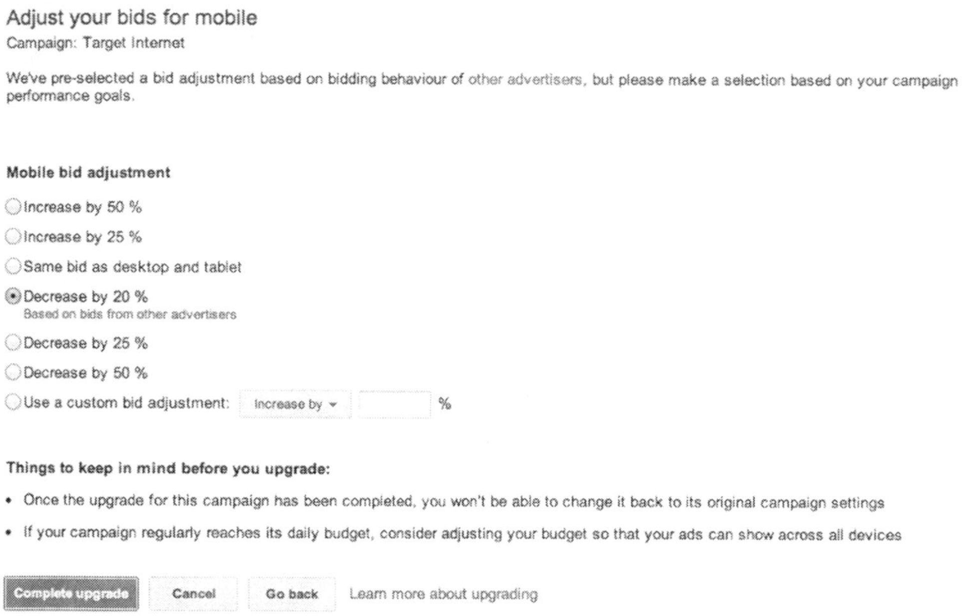

Adjust your bids for mobile
Campaign: Target Internet

We've pre-selected a bid adjustment based on bidding behaviour of other advertisers, but please make a selection based on your campaign performance goals.

Mobile bid adjustment

○ Increase by 50 %

○ Increase by 25 %

○ Same bid as desktop and tablet

◉ Decrease by 20 %
 Based on bids from other advertisers

○ Decrease by 25 %

○ Decrease by 50 %

○ Use a custom bid adjustment: Increase by ▾ ____ %

Things to keep in mind before you upgrade:

• Once the upgrade for this campaign has been completed, you won't be able to change it back to its original campaign settings

• If your campaign regularly reaches its daily budget, consider adjusting your budget so that your ads can show across all devices

[Complete upgrade]   [Cancel]   [Go back]   Learn more about upgrading

Within Google and their new Enhanced Campaigns, you can also adjust your bids according to context-based information such as mobile devices and time of day. For example you may decide that mobile searches are more likely to convert into business so may be willing to pay more for a mobile click. You may also find that mobile searches are less competitive than desktop searches and that you can actually decrease your bids slightly (see Figure 12.13). My experience is that in most cases currently, you can decrease your bids by 20 per cent and have no impact on your traffic levels, but you need to test and this will vary across different keywords.

This ability to target by device is incredibly under-used currently, especially when you consider that in many cases a mobile search has a higher likelihood of converting than a desktop search.

Within Google AdWords you also have the options to set rules-based bidding, meaning that you do things like automatically adjust your bid (within a certain range) to always keep your ad in a certain position. This can help you automate your bidding to factor changes in competition levels.

PPC considerations

Beyond the fundamentals of PPC, there are some other things we need to consider when planning our campaigns that can have a significant impact on what value we get for our budgets.

Ongoing management and optimization

To get the most out of your PPC budgets your campaigns will need to be closely monitored, tested and adjusted on an ongoing basis. Levels of competition can change, and bids will need to change accordingly. You may find that certain keywords are working well and that others, although driving traffic, are not converting into business. Again, you will need to adjust your campaigns accordingly. This means that as well as considering the cost of your PPC budgets you need to factor in the time or cost of managing your campaigns effectively as well. We'll discuss using agencies for PPC management further in a moment.

Quality scoring

The Google AdWords system is particularly focussed on rewarding campaigns that are highly targeted and give relevant results for searchers. They do this by factoring in a quality score when deciding what ads to show and how high up the page those ads should be displayed. Quality scores take into account a number of factors but look at things like the click-through rate (CTR) of your ad to signify its relevance. That means that ads that are seen as being relevant are given a boost in their positioning and you can actually have your ad appearing above the ad of somebody else who is actually paying more per click than you.

Other quality factors include having the word/phrase that was searched for actually in your ad and on the landing page that you are sending searchers through to. The more relevant your ad, the better your quality score and the more visibility you get for your budget. It also means that Google is rewarding relevant ads; that in turn means that searchers see PPC ads as more relevant generally; searchers should in turn click on the ads more, thus making Google more money. Clever stuff.

Conversion tracking

As with any digital marketing activity, we need to understand what impact it is having on our bottom line. We'll discuss the idea of a 'conversion' further in Chapter 18, but most PPC systems give you some ability to track beyond a click and see what happens afterwards. After all, all the traffic in the world is useless if the visitors to our site all leave immediately upon arrival.

Working with PPC agencies

Agencies can help you get the most from your PPC budgets by planning and setting up your campaigns effectively and then managing your campaigns on an ongoing basis. They can also add additional cost and bring little benefit. If you are going to work with an agency you need to be very clear on what value they provide and if this is giving you a positive return on investment (ROI).

From my experience of working with lots of agencies, and having run a search agency, there are a couple of key things to look out for: payment terms and campaign management.

Payment terms

Far too many PPC agencies charge on a 'percentage of spend' basis. So, for example, you pay them 20 per cent of what you are spending on your PPC clicks. This approach makes no sense for a couple of reasons. First of all, more money doesn't necessarily mean more work to manage that budget. It may do, but it's really down to how that budget is being spent. Secondly, for an agency there is no incentive to save you money and reduce your budget if that is then going to reduce their fee.

Another issue to consider is campaign ownership and handover fees. What I mean by this is being very careful of contracts with PPC agencies that state that they own the campaign data and/or there is a handover fee for your campaign. This can mean you are charged to set up a campaign, but when you cease working with the agency you either have to pay them to hand over the account or start again from scratch. It can also mean that if you part company with the agency that ran your PPC, you no longer have access to the data collected during that campaign, such as which ads/key phrases were performing best, and you need to start the test and learn process from scratch.

Campaign management

A final consideration is how much work are you actually getting for your budget? Many PPC campaigns are managed for a monthly fee, but when the campaign is up and running successfully, it is very easy to sit back and just let things tick over without doing any work. For this reason, instead of a monthly bill that just reads 'campaign management', you need a breakdown of what work has actually been done. The Google AdWords system can actually track all changes made to a campaign over any given period, which can help you get to the bottom of what work has actually been done. Even when getting these work breakdowns, look out for the catch-all 'keyword research'. It is a valid activity, but you need to understand what keyword research was actually done and what was the output.

Mobile SEO and PPC working together

As we can see, there are some very specific considerations when looking at mobile search. We also need to consider how SEO and PPC can work together effectively within mobile marketing. My first point on this is always that PPC on mobile devices is even more important than it is on desktop devices. This is because of the much smaller screen sizes at play, and the greater amount of this space that paid search gets over organic search. It is also because many mobile searches are in relation to a commercial need, and, as we have explored, PPC results are most likely to be clicked on when the search term indicates high commercial intent.

I'm often asked whether you should bother with PPC advertising if you are already ranking number 1 for a search term in the organic search results. The only way to truly get an answer to that question is by testing it. Look at your results with and without PPC running and you can answer the question precisely. This testing is even more necessary with mobile search, because of the different user focus and motivations. You will certainly get some cannibalization, that is people clicking on your paid ads that would have clicked on your organic search results, but you need to understand what additional traffic you can get and then look at how PPC and SEO traffic convert differently.

Mobile search: conclusions

PPC campaigns targeted at mobile users are currently under-utilized, and clearly this gives us an opportunity to get more from our budgets by targeting effectively. SEO for mobile is also under-utilized, due to the number of sites not being optimized for mobile devices and the search engines becoming increasingly aware of this. This means that effectively planned and implemented mobile search campaigns can be one of our most important business drivers.

Mobile advertising

13

We are going to start this chapter with some definitions and some warnings. Mobile advertising is fundamentally about various forms of banner advertising including video ads. The reality is that paid search is a form of mobile advertising, but we have discussed this topic as part of the search section of this book. Another issue is that due to the amount of different creative options, the term banner advertising doesn't really cover all of the different things we can do with mobile ads.

Now let's move to the warnings. We have already discussed how screen space is at a premium on mobile devices; that we have slow internet connections much of the time; and that we are often very objective and action-focussed when using mobile devices. All of these factors mean that any online advertising that slows down my experience or gets in my way is likely to be at best ineffective, and at worst counter-productive and damaging to a brand.

Actually, this is probably the easiest aspect of mobile marketing to waste your budget on and carry out ineffective campaigns. This is because banner ads are the easiest part of mobile marketing (and digital marketing more broadly) to understand from a traditional advertising perspective. So, many traditional marketers' approach to digital has been to create some print/TV ads and then create some digital equivalent of these in a banner format. This approach is generally poorly targeted and not adjusted for the digital channel. Much of the blame for this lies with agencies that don't really understand digital.

The positive side of online advertising is that we now have a wide range of creative and targeting options that can improve the effectiveness of our ads along with the analytics and metrics to judge their success.

Mobile advertising objectives

Just as with any other aspect of mobile marketing we should start by clearly defining what our actual end objectives are and how mobile advertising is going to contribute to these goals. The reason this is even more important to define when considering mobile ads is because of the way they are often priced and measured.

Most online advertising is sold on a cost per mille (CPM) basis. This basically means that you pay a certain fee every time your ad is shown a thousand times. This means you are paying for display, not for clicks, and certainly not for results. This isn't the only option, but it is the most common. This means it's very easy to waste budget on views of your ad by the completely wrong audience.

Your ad being shown once is called an 'impression'. If I hit 'refresh' 10 times on a page with an ad on it that will be 10 ad impressions. Also, if a page loads that my ad is on, but the ad is below the fold (below the part of the page that I can see without scrolling down), and the user doesn't scroll down the page, the ad will still register an impression even though nobody saw it. The impression also doesn't tell you how long the user was actually on the page that the ad was shown on. This 'page view duration' is referred to as 'dwell time', and even if my dwell time was half a second, if the ad loaded, an impression gets counted. We clearly need to look carefully at what we are paying for.

Another challenge with online advertising is that results are often measured on a click-through rate (CTR) basis. The reality though, is that even if we get clicks it doesn't mean that the visitor that drives to my site will necessarily carry out the action that we want them to. They may leave my site as soon as they arrive. Equally, somebody that doesn't click on my ads may interact with them in some way and go on to make a purchase. We need to find better ways than CTR to measure the success of an ad.

App advertising

As well as the options for advertising on mobile sites, we also need to consider ads within apps. This may be from the perspective of running ad campaigns in appropriate apps that are used by my target audience, but it may be from the perspective of making money by placing ads within our apps.

The ad formats are generally very similar for mobile sites and for apps and we'll look at these when we look at the creative options available to us.

Both Apple and Google have mobile ad platforms to allow you to sell advertising space in your apps (iAds and AdMob respectively) and on both iOS and Android you can integrate ads from a wide variety of different ad networks (which we'll discuss later). All of these solutions generally work by automatically placing ads within your apps (in the locations you have developed in the app) and then giving you a share of the revenue made from the ads.

If you want to advertise within apps, then there are a number of different ad networks you could go to (again, more on this later) or you could approach an app owner directly to negotiate a deal.

Ad networks vs media owners

An ad network manages the advertising space on a number of different mobile properties that may include both mobile sites and apps. These ad networks may also manage advertising space on desktop sites. They offer a range of targeting options and then place your ads within the sites they manage according to your targeting criteria. Different ad networks have different targeting criteria, which can vary from fairly basic options like category matching (automotive, finance etc) all the way through to things like behavioural targeting (which we'll explore when we look at targeting options).

Generally ad networks charge a fee and then share some of this with the owner of the location the ads are shown in. They provide the technology for placing the ads, the account management to the advertisers and provide some form of reporting for all parties involved.

Ad networks are the reason for there being standard sizes and types of ads. This means you can create an ad once and it can be run across multiple properties (mobile sites and apps) without the need to redesign every time.

Internet Advertising Bureau

The Internet Advertising Bureau (IAB) is the trade association for online and mobile advertising. It promotes growth and best practice for advertisers, agencies and media owners. It has sites for regions around the world sharing best practice and defines the standards for sizes and types of ads. This includes the various types of mobile ads and things like how big they should be in regard to screen size, file size and so on.

The global website can be found below, but they also have local market sites which are also listed here: **http://www.iab.net**.

Rather than going to an ad network, you could go directly to a media owner. A media owner in mobile marketing is somebody that owns a site or app (or even an e-mail list) that you may wish to advertise on. Going directly to a media owner has the advantage of knowing exactly where and how your ads will be shown (this often isn't true when using ad networks because much ad placement is 'blind placement', meaning you set the targeting criteria but don't get to choose the exact sites your ads show on). The disadvantage is that very often you are targeting one site or app at a time and they don't have the targeting technologies available via the ad networks. They may also be limited in the types of creative options they can offer and the reporting facilities they can give you.

Targeting options

Different ad networks offer different types of ad targeting, and I've summarized the most common ones below. A single network normally doesn't offer all of the different targeting options, and different networks will be able to place advertising on different websites. You may need to work with multiple ad networks to achieve your campaign objectives.

Location

Place your ads based on location-based criteria such as country, city and distance from a physical location. This option can often also be used to exclude as well as include an area.

Device and OS

Place ads based on device and operating system. Some networks also allow you to choose by version of operating system.

Carrier

Ad placement by network provider. This can also allow you to choose between a WiFi- and carrier-based internet connection (based on the fact you may only want to target ads when users have a fast internet connection).

Demographic

Target by criteria such as age and gender. This may be based on users having registered their details or it may be based on some sort of modelling, in which case it's worth understanding how this data is modelled and how likely the data is to be accurate.

Category

One of the simplest forms of targeting, based on category of the content within the site or app. For example, automotive, finance etc.

Content matched

The content of the page the ad is being placed on is read, and ads are matched based on that content. This can be effective, but just because I am reading a news story about pirates, doesn't mean I want to buy a boat!

Behavioural

There are lots of different approaches to behavioural targeting, but generally these rely on being able to see a user's behaviour across a website (or number of websites) and then targeting ads accordingly. I may be looking at an automotive website, but if I have just been on three websites looking at credit card deals, then it is perfectly valid to show me an ad for credit cards on the automotive website.

Re-targeting

This allows you to show ads to people who have visited your site before. So for example if I visit your site but don't buy anything, I could then be shown ads for your site on other websites.

Guide to mobile ad networks

The mobile ad network environment is massively fragmented with new entrants with new technologies joining the market all of the time.
The team over at MobiThinking are doing a great job of summarizing the market and updating this information regularly: **http://mobithinking.com/ mobile-ad-network-guide**.

Creative options

This is where things start to get very interesting. The number of different creative options for mobile ads is exploding. We've highlighted a few of the more common options below and pointed out some great resources for getting some creative inspiration (a black and white book doesn't really do interactive mobile advertising full justice!).

Banners

Images can be displayed with or without animation, and users can 'tap' the banner to be taken to a variety of destinations.

Expandable

Expands an ad to cover the full screen upon a tap, without removing the user from the app or mobile browser experience.

Interstitial

Displays full screen-rich media ads either at app- or mobile-browser launch or in between content pages.

Video

Various options to place video before/after/during other video content or within other rich media formats.

The IAB 'Mobile Rising Stars Ad Units' (see Figure 13.1) highlights some of the new and highly interactive mobile ad formats, and generally gives videos to show how they work in action. These ad formats have great creative opportunities but aren't necessarily widely available.

FIGURE 13.1   IAB Mobile Rising Stars Ad Units (www.iab.net)

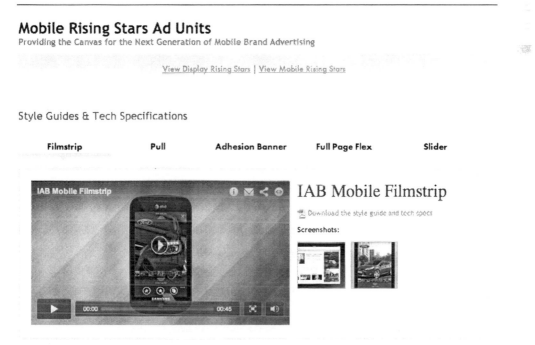

Mobile Phone Creative Guidelines

The IAB have also partnered with the Mobile Marketing Association (MMA) to create the Mobile Phone Creative Guidelines, which provides standards and guidance on using the most common mobile advertising formats: **http://www.iab.net/mobileguidelines**

Mobile ad features

As well as the dizzying array of targeting and creative options, there is also a growing range of ad features and functionality that can be used to encourage users to take an action after seeing/interacting with an ad. We looked at a few of these options when we looked at paid search ads, considering options like click-to-call and click-to-map. Display ads give even more options, with options like click-to-install (allowing users to install an app by clicking on an ad) and even deep-linking into a particular screen within an app.

As well as these features which are becoming more standardized, rich media ad formats can offer a huge range of ad functionality.

Apple provides its iAd Gallery app (see Figure 13.2) to demonstrate some of the options available on its iAd platform, offering a range of creative mobile ad examples. Google offers its own creative gallery on the Creative Sandbox website: **http://www.creativesandbox.com**.

Ad reporting and analytics

Most ad networks will provide a range of reporting tools, but ideally we should integrate our advertising data with our mobile and app analytics so we can get an integrated view of our mobile marketing efforts.

An initial step is to make sure that all of our mobile ads are tagged with an analytics tracking code. This allows us to identify any traffic coming from our mobile ads to our sites and apps and then track this

FIGURE 13.2   Apple's iAd Gallery app (http://advertising.apple.com)

iAd Gallery

By Apple

Open iTunes to buy and download apps.

View More By This Developer

Description

Great ads. On-demand. In your pocket. The iAd Gallery is a celebration of advertising, featuring iAd campaigns from some of the world's best brands and their advertising agencies. The iAd Gallery gives you easy access to a selection of the fun and informative ads that have run in some of your favorite apps. Use the Browse feature to discover ads

Apple Web Site ▸   iAd Gallery Support ▸   Application License Agreement ▸   ...More

What's New in Version 1.2

• Supports compatibility with iOS 6.

This update is recommended for all iAd Gallery users.

View In iTunes

Free

Category: Business
Updated: Sep 19, 2012
Version: 1.2
Size: 1.7 MB
Seller: Apple Inc.
© 2011
Rated 12+ for the following:
Infrequent/Mild Alcohol,
Tobacco, or Drug Use or
References

Requirements: Compatible with
iPhone, iPod touch, and iPad.
Requires iOS 4.2.6 or later.

Customer Ratings

Current Version:
★★★✦ 20 Ratings
All Versions:
★★★★ 252 Ratings

More iPhone Apps by Apple

iMovie
View In iTunes ▸

iPhone Screenshots

BMW
X3

American Express
Zync
Agency: Ogilvy, New York, NY

TAP TO MEET ZYNC
FROM AMERICAN EXPRESS®

Tap Banner To View iAd

American Express Zync is the card you can customize. Pick point packs that can double rewards for the stuff you care about, like music, travel or green products. Watch TV spots featuring tunes from Andrew Bird, The Antlers and Passion Pit, or click to call American Express and apply for a Zync card

---

through to conversion. We outlined instructions of how to do this for Google Analytics in Chapter 18 of this book.

Taking things a stage further, Google now allows you to import data from other ad networks and platforms into Google Analytics so you can compare and contrast data in one place. This functionality can be found under the Traffic Sources reports and is currently titled Cost Analysis.

Google Analytics and single customer view

Google realizes the importance of having all of our sources of data from digital marketing in one place so we can effectively analyse and manipulate the data to make smarter marketing decisions. Cost Analysis and various announcements made recently demonstrate Google's intentions to maintain Analytics as the place to get your single customer view, allowing users to bring in and connect more third-party data sources into the Google environment.

Mobile advertising: conclusions

The mobile advertising market is currently highly fragmented with a huge range of ad targeting, features and creative options. Just like any form of banner advertising, the results of campaigns are highly variable based on the options used and the overall effectiveness of approach. For this reason any online advertising efforts should be carefully considered and tied back to business objectives, with a clear methodology for tracking and measuring results put in place from the outset.

The varied, and often highly interactive, creative options available are very impressive. However, if we go back to our initial concerns about screen space, internet speed and user objectives, we need to ask some very searching questions before making assumption about the effectiveness of any mobile advertising campaigns.

Augmented reality (AR) and real-world integration

14

According to Wikipedia, augmented reality (AR) is 'a live, direct or indirect, view of a physical, real-world environment whose elements are *augmented* by computer-generated sensory input such as sound, video, graphics or GPS data'. And herein lies the first problem of AR: it can mean lots of different things and covers a fairly wide range of apps and functionality. We'll get the opinion of an industry thought leader later in this chapter, but let's try and simplify things a little.

In simple terms, AR overlays information on top of what we see in the real world. This can be done via the camera and screen on a mobile device, or by using some customized solution like Google Glass. (Figure 14.1 shows a screenshot of an early video from the Google Glass project demonstrating the core concepts of AR.) There are a range of apps that offer AR, from apps that help you find your nearest pub by overlaying geographic location data onto what your phone camera sees, through to more advanced and integrated solutions like Blippar that we'll discuss later.

Blippar is one of many AR apps available and it allows you to 'blipp', which basically means scanning an object with a mobile device or phone, using an app to recognize the object, and then delivering some form of defined interactive experience. For example, the screenshots in Figures 14.2 and 14.3 show a print magazine that has been set up with Blippar. This means the app will recognize various

FIGURE 14.1   Google Glass project: early video
(www.google.com/glass)

FIGURE 14.2   Using AR to bridge between online and offline
(www.blippar.com)

pages of the magazine, and in this case deliver an interactive game. This requires no QR code or similar but does require the object being scanned to be set up within the Blippar environment. As a marketer, if you wanted your poster, product or magazine page to be scannable, you would approach Blippar to arrange this.

Adoption levels

They key challenge with apps like Blippar, that allow you to scan real-world objects and launch some form of interactive experience

FIGURE 14.3 'Blipped' magazine page launching interactive experience (www.blippar.com)

(without the need for a QR code or similar), is user adoption. Unless a certain percentage of mobile consumers have got the app, it's unlikely that marketers will start to use it extensively. It's also unlikely a large percentage of mobile consumers will start using the app, unless marketers are using it widely. Classic chicken-and-egg problem and one that has been faced by many technologies over the years. Time will tell what the final outcome will be, but a few things are clear.

AR offers huge creative potential and immensely useful functionality.

The Google Glass reaction

Google Glass is the wearable AR (and much more) product from Google that you can find out more about here: **http://www.google.com/glass/**.

We've mentioned Google Glass a number of times in this book already, and at the time of publishing, the device seems to be getting two very distinct reactions: one of great enthusiasm for the functionality and usefulness it can offer (I definitely find myself in that camp); and another group feeling that it is a step toward dehumanizing ourselves, integrating with technology too much, with much fear about the social implications. We'll leave these discussions about the social issues alone for now, but what is clear is that wide usage of AR is coming and it's coming very soon.

Location-based services

Before we get too carried away with AR and Google Glass, let's go back to basics a little bit. A wide range of location-based services help make mobile sites and apps more useful already. Google Maps knows where I am and can give me step-by-step route guidance based on my current location. Airport Angel can tell me which airline lounges I can use nearest to my current location. Facebook knows where I am and allows me to log the location of my posts.

These location-based services are part of the real-world integration that is giving us such great functionality, and actually what we are really talking about is a range of technologies working together. Most smartphones now have both GPS for working out your location, and a gyroscope for working out the direction you're facing and the angle you're holding your phone at. This means we can create great games that take our physical feedback or apps that point us in the right direction. The bottom line is that, as most mobile devices have this functionality in common, developers will use it. If a particular functionality is limited, adoption of apps using it will be limited. We'll look at this problem again when we consider near field communication technology.

Location check-ins

Foursquare was the app that moved the idea of a location-based check-in into the mainstream. A check-in is just tagging yourself as being in a certain physical location. The app allowed you to check into a particular location and used gamification to encourage usage. By carrying out check-ins at certain locations, in a certain order or over a number of times, you could earn badges. You could also become the 'mayor' of a location by checking in there more than anybody else. Lots of people loved this gamification. Lots more people thought it was futile and didn't see how it could be used for business purposes.

Foursquare has now been transformed into a more business- and utility-focussed app (see Figure 14.4), allowing brands to set up location-based interaction with an audience and helping users to share location-based data, like restaurant reviews and recommendations.

The key challenge for an app like Foursquare is that both Facebook and Google, much bigger players than themselves, are offering very similar functionality on platforms that people are already using. Why download another app when I can do everything in Facebook? Again this raises questions about adoption levels and uniqueness of product offering. Privacy is also an issue that we need to consider at this stage as well. What are the consequences of sharing my physical location? Do I want Facebook to know that about me as well? From a marketer's point of view, all of this data is hugely valuable, but I need to make sure that I have a clear proposition (as discussed in Part One of this book) that tells the user what they are getting in exchange for the data they are sharing. I also need the consumer's trust more than ever to make sure they are willing to share data in the first place.

FIGURE 14.4   Foursquare: location-based check-ins create brand engagement (www.foursquare.com/hmusa)

Follow us on *foursquare* to get exclusive offers & tips

H&M

Follow us & check in on foursquare to unlock H&M tips and deals in your city. H&M offers fashion and quality at affordable prices for women, men and children. The collections are comprehensive, and new merchandise arrives in the store every day. In this way customers can always find something new and create their own personal style show more...

LIKE H&M

Likes (335,191 total)

Photos

See all 45 photos

H&M locations

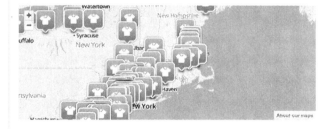

Recent updates

H&M at 5 nearby locations
Chula Vista, CA

Mother's Day is around the corner. Treat your mom to the perfect gift from H&M!

FIGURE 14.5   Foursquare: location-based check-ins create brand engagement (www.foursquare.com)

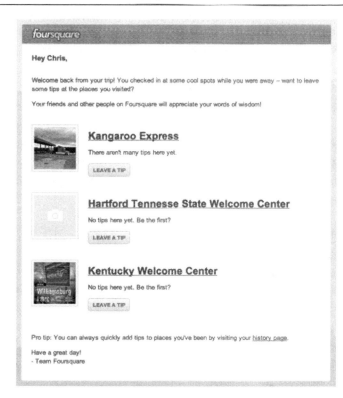

Blippar and the future of real-world integration

I was lucky enough to speak to Jessica Butcher, co-founder and CMO of Blippar, about the company and how she sees the current and future AR market. Jessica was named as one of *Fortune Magazine*'s 'Top 10 Most Powerful Women Entrepreneurs' of 2012 and winner of the Iris award (tech entrepreneur category) at the 'NatWest everywoman Awards'.

How do you sum up Blippar to those without any knowledge of AR?

We hate the term 'AR'! It's techie, nerdy and non-specific – it's become a catch-all term for anything that uses the phone's camera – previously used to describe geo-located bubbles of information which appear over your screen showing you where your nearest 'x' is – and now shifted to describe a totally different image-recognition technology. We prefer 'visual discovery' and better still 'blipping'. What's thrilling about what's happening In this space is that any image, photo, logo, printed page or product can be recognized through the eye/camera of the phone and trigger a powerful, content-rich experience. Simply 'look' at something, and instantly extract information or entertainment from it. That content doesn't have to be 'floating' or 'hovering' over the image as if 'in' the real world – it could be an exclusive video that plays, a web page that opens, a train timetable that is triggered, a recipe or coupon that is downloaded, or an instant competition win. Anything!

Blippar is that 'eye'. It is a mobile platform, downloaded as an app which provides a single lens through which anything that is blippable can be unlocked – a magazine, newspaper, billboard, in-store sign, product package or photo! Every new campaign or content partnership that is attracted to use the platform assists in its growth – plus it has access to the already acquired audience (1.5 million as of December 2012, and growing rapidly).

What has been the significant change in your market in recent times?

More players with a multitude of technologies and business models. Less 'wow for wow's sake' and finally (thankfully!) more focus on the actual applications of the technology, conversion rates and success metrics. Finally, our partners are appreciating that the success of this, as a new behavioural medium, is less about the tech per se and more about the quality of the content experience that is delivered through it.

High conversion data is now coming through strongly showing that the tech is ready now, not just 'one to watch' for the future.

What has been the biggest challenge for growth with Blippar?

Having enough content to pique the interest of consumers. We've focussed on quality of experience over quantity of interactive 'markers' – in an effort to learn about best practice and how the consumer wants to engage with this as a new medium. Next year is all about taking this learning and driving the quantity side of things!

Where do you see the future of Blippar and of AR generally?

It will become habitual to 'blipp' the physical world around us to extract more: more information, utility, offers, value and entertainment. Magazines will be read phone-in-hand, bus stops and public transports routinely 'scanned' for entertainment and content on-the-go, and much, much more.

What is your favourite app other than Blippar and why?

Shazam. It's the ears of the phone, whereas we're the eyes. Great app, great business and model.

CASE STUDY   VH1 and Foursquare

Industry

Entertainment, non-profit

Location

USA

Marketing objectives

- brand awareness;

- drive online donations.

Their challenge

VH1 have been running their 'Save the Music' programme since 1997 which aims to provide schoolchildren with access to long-term, sustainable musical education initiatives. In 2012 the foundation was looking for a way to boost awareness, raise additional funds and utilize social media and mobile to increase advocacy.

Their solution

VH1 teamed up with Foursquare who created a specific music supporter badge which users unlocked whenever they checked into a music venue across the country. Each time a user checked in, VH1 donated $1 to the campaign in order to achieve the goal of $35,000 which would go to a nominated school. The campaign would run until the target was reached at which point the badge would be retired.

Their results

The campaign was launched in March 2012 and raised its target of $35,000 within three months. It has been one of the most successful campaigns run by VH1 for its Save the Music Foundation, as well as being a trailblazing campaign demonstrating brands leveraging social media for social change activities.

What's good about it

Not enough is being done or is understood by non-profit brands about how they can leverage social media platforms for increased awareness of campaign messages. This collaboration demonstrates how partnerships between commercial and charitable companies work really well.

The campaign not only raised the profile of the foundation's mission, but also cemented Foursquare as a tool that goes beyond just the fun factor of check-ins and earning badges. At the same time, it was easy for users to engage as they weren't asked to change their interaction habits but merely carry on with what they were doing while being given the opportunity to feel good about supporting a cause.

What they said about it

It felt good to leverage emerging platforms like Foursquare to not only build our brand, but support real actions that have bigger, life-impacting effects. We're reminding people that at our core we celebrate celebrities and artists for doing good, and are constantly getting ourselves involved as well.

Nigel Cox-Hagan, EVP of Creative and Marketing, VH1

Quick Response (QR) codes

Quick Response (QR) codes allow you to scan a square code using your mobile device, which can then trigger some behaviour within your device. Normally this means doing something like launching a website, a page for a web app or a map (we'll explore what we can do with QR codes later). Figure 15.1 is a typical QR code which, when scanned, will take you to the website that accompanies this book.

Many of us will be familiar with the concept of QR codes (don't worry if you're not, we'll get there in a moment), but the most often asked question about them is: does anybody actually use them? The answer is both yes and no. Lots of people do use them, use is growing, but it is still a relatively small percentage of our audience in many cases. What I will try and show you in this chapter though is that it's more about using QR codes effectively that impacts how much they are used, rather than how much the general population is using them.

FIGURE 15.1 QR code for *Mobile Marketing*

Barcodes have been in use for years as a way to quickly grab product details. A standard barcode can only contain numerical data on a horizontal axis. So if you want your barcode to transfer more data, you need to make it longer. This very quickly becomes very impractical.

Enter the 2D code, a system for compressing barcode data across the horizontal **and** vertical axes. These 2D barcodes have evolved to convey a lot more data in a smaller space than their earlier one-dimensional cousins, so loved by the supermarket checkout. There are a number of 2D code formats that have been developed, but the QR code format is the most widely adopted and supported of these formats.

Some of the other formats of 2D codes out there are in fact technically superior to QR codes, but it's really about adoption and how many people actually have a scanner to read the codes. We'll see this occurring as a common theme in some of the technology sections of this book. Until the adoption of software or hardware is sufficient to make the technology generally usable, we don't tend to use the technology. However, if we don't use the technology, developers, marketers and handset manufacturers tend not to adopt the technology. QR codes have got past the initial chicken-and-egg situation, but the question now is whether users really care enough to use them.

One of the major problems of QR codes is that you need to get out your device, launch an app to read QR codes and then scan the code. Although this isn't a huge effort, you really need to have a persuasive value proposition to make people do this when they are being bombarded with marketing messages competing for their attention. But, let's take a step back and look at the fundamentals of the QR code format.

QR codes in perspective

The QR code format was created back in 1994, and can handle a wide range of different types of data, such as numeric and alphabetic characters, Kanji, Kana, Hiragana, symbols, binary and control codes. Up to 7,089 characters can be encoded in one symbol. They can be read in any direction by the scanner at high speed. They also contain a level of error correction, allowing the code to be interpreted correctly if it is in any way damaged or dirty (handy if, for example, you are in a dusty warehouse or are reading the code with a poor quality phone camera from a distance). When you create the code you can control the level of error correction, with options of between 7 per cent and 30 per cent of the image data missing, depending on the correction level you choose. The codes are an open format and can be created by anyone without charge and the standards are internationally agreed and accepted.

You can read more about QR codes at QRcode.com, an excellent resource created by Denso Wave who created and own the format but allow its free use: **http://www.qrcode.com**.

QR code drawbacks

The format sounds great, but there are a couple of drawbacks. In order to store a lot of data in the code, the QR code's dimensions grow. The format is measured in modules (the small squares they are built from). It allows for codes as small as 21 × 21 modules up to 177 × 177 modules (the maximum size allows for 4,296 alphanumeric characters if you are using error correction). The error correction percentage, if increased, will reduce the amount of data you can store in the code. QR codes also have a slightly 'retro 8-bit pixelated graphics' quality about them, without using colour. You can change the colours used from black and white as long as the contrast is there for the reader to detect the pattern. We'll talk more about improving the visual aspects of your QR code in a moment.

The main drawback is usage. What a lot of the adoption reports and statistics miss is: just because you have scanned a QR code once doesn't mean you do it on a regular basis. More on that later, but what it really comes down to is offering enough value to make the effort of scanning worthwhile.

Practical applications

So we have a code system, and we can embed data in it. So what? The key benefit is shown clearly in the name: quick response. The ability to drive an immediate response or action is central to their use in mobile, and QR codes can help us bridge the gap between the real world and the online world.

Initially retailers started using barcodes to make reading product details and prices fast and efficient. Before barcodes were in wide use, retailers relied on price labels to read and input prices at the till, and there was no direct way to measure what stock had been sold. It was painfully slow, with huge margins for input error that could be costly. Inputting prices in this way would be unthinkable in today's retail environments. However, we operate in a very similar environment in the marketing world every day.

As you travel around, there is no shortage of advertisers and retailers making use of long website addresses to direct customers to their online offerings. Attempts are made to make these as memorable as possible, but have you ever bothered to actually enter these long strings of letters into a mobile phone while you are out and about? Much like the barcode, QR codes offer a quick solution whenever fast interaction is needed and can help bridge 'traditional' media and online.

QR codes certainly aren't limited to getting someone to a website and we'll explore how they are used most effectively in a moment.

QR code adoption

I'll start by saying that a global view of QR code adoption is patchy at best, and much of the research that has been done has looked at slightly different things and asked slightly different questions. I've highlighted what I believe are the most important trends below. You must remember, however, that just because your country shows a particular adoption percentage, it doesn't mean your target audience is going to reflect that percentage.

A number of figures show continuing significant growth in usage over the past two years, with global growth averaged out at 381 per cent between 2011 and 2013 (QRCodeStuff.com, 2013). However, figures like this can still be misleading if not seen in context. We need to understand the actual percentage of the population using QR codes and see how regularly they are using them.

An eMarketer report shows that around 25 per cent of the adult population in the United States has used a QR code in the last year, but that growth rates are slowing and this was only expected to rise to around 27 per cent in late 2014 (eMarketer, 2013). This contrasts with figures published by Comscore, showing European adoption at around 11–19 per cent of smartphone users in late 2012 (Comscore, 2012). Throughout Asia the story is very different, with adoption averaging around 50 per cent of smartphone users (some samples are showing China as high as 70 per cent) using QR codes in the past year (AIP, 2013).

In regard to which devices people are using, there is a report showing increasing numbers of iPhone users starting to scan QR codes in 2013, with growth from 43 per cent of all scans in 2011 through to around 59 per cent in 2013 (QRCodeStuff.com, 2013). The rise has been explained by both growing awareness of QR codes, but also the increasing adoption of QR scanning capability and sophistication of apps.

The most important thing to understand about QR codes

Hopefully that heading got your attention. The reality is that QR adoption is growing, but it still represents a relatively low percentage of the population. I have been running a reasonably unscientific study for the past three months (raise-of-hand questions at 32 training sessions across six countries in Europe, North America and Asia) and have seen around 25 per cent use by smartphone users, but only around 10 per cent stating they use them regularly (Target Internet, 2013).

However, let's put this in perspective by looking at something slightly different. Paid-per-click (PPC) ads in Google are the text ads you normally get at the top and right-hand side of the page. According to lots of data, more than 90 per cent of clicks go to the organic search and not to these paid ads (Search Engine Watch, 2013). So should we forget about PPC ads? Absolutely not, because data shows that actually these ads get more than 64 per cent of clicks when the search word shows 'high commercial intent' (WordStream, 2013), basically meaning that when you are looking to buy something you are more likely to click on a PPC ad. What this shows is that if you use the right technology, at the right time and in the right way, it can work, and this doesn't necessarily fit in with standard usage.

The reality is that people will use QR codes if you give them a strong enough value proposition (even people who haven't used them before or don't use them regularly). The other key question is: is this the most appropriate way to try and drive a response? We'll also take a look at things like near field communication (NFC) and augmented reality (AR). The reality is that these technologies may offer superior functionality, but they have even lower adoption rates than QR codes currently.

Latest QR code adoption figures

As with all books, by the time you read this, the data here will be slightly out of date. For this reason you can find links to the latest QR code adoption figures and a huge range of resources on QR codes that we didn't have space to print on our website: **http://www.targetinternet.com/mobilemarketing/**.

Or you could just scan the QR code in Figure 15.1 at the beginning of this chapter!

Making your QR code beautiful

One of the main complaints about QR codes is their ugliness and what impact this has on your print materials or wherever else you are placing them. There are, however, a few things you can do about this.

FIGURE 15.2 QR code with embedded image and gradient of colour (QR Code Monkey)

You can change the size of your QR code to embed a shape within it, change its colour and even apply gradients. All of these effects can be achieved for free and you can see an example in Figure 15.2 generated on the excellent **http://www.qrcode-monkey.com/**.

You can take this design process a step further and implement your QR code into an image. There are a number of tools that can do this, and some graphic design companies can offer this as a bespoke service. The example in Figure 15.3 shows a QR code that links to a Facebook page, with the Facebook logo embedded into it. This code was generated

FIGURE 15.3 QR code with image merged into the code (VisualLead.com)

using VisualLead, a website that allows you to generate image-based QR codes. It's not free but the cost is very low and you get extensive reporting once your code is generated: **http://www.visualead.com/**.

Practical guide to using QR codes in the real world

Before you rush off in a fit of enthusiasm and start covering everything you create in QR codes, there are a few things you should always remember:

- Your customers will be accessing the resource you are linking to on a mobile device. Make sure the resource you direct them to is designed and optimized for mobile.

- Using a QR code, although quick, is still a hassle. Make sure you are adequately rewarding the customer for making the effort with something really worthwhile.

- Keep the amount of data you encode as short as possible to keep the QR simple.

Generating QR codes

If you are looking for a code generator, there are hundreds to choose from, but one of my favourites is **http://delivr.com/qr-code-generator**.

You can also use the Google URL shortener **http://goo.gl** to create shortened URLs (mostly used in Twitter to avoid using up all of your 140 characters with a link). The nice thing about this is that you'll then receive reports on usage of your code, and as it's a Google product it's very reliable and fast. A quick tip with this is that after you've generated your shortened URL, you can look at the 'details' and see the QR code. If you then click on the code, you'll see it showing in your browser. Somewhere in the URL for the code you'll see some text that reads '150 × 150'. You can change this to read '500 × 500' for example and get a much larger version of your code, which will be useful when using the code in print ads, which are generally printed at higher resolution than are used online.

Going beyond web links

Obviously, links to online resources for mobile users are a quick win but you can do a lot more with QR codes. It's possible to embed contact details into the codes. Want to make sure your customers can get in touch without having to input long telephone numbers and e-mail addresses? Why not embed a link to your contact details in a QR code so they can instantly e-mail or call you? Many QR code generators make this very easy to do, and the one at QRCode Monkey is excellent: **http://www.qrcode-monkey.com/**.

If you are embedding actual web addresses, always make sure you include the full http:// part of the address. This should ensure that most devices will recognize the type of information they are being given and launch the page automatically. If you miss it out, the user is very often just shown the link as text.

The future of QR codes

The reality is that many people are predicting the death of QR codes, and there was a real trend to dismiss them at the end of 2012 when making predictions for 2013. In fact, we've seen growth of their usage in all global markets. This doesn't mean that everyone is using them, but usage levels are significant enough to mean that if you employ QR codes effectively they can be an excellent way of driving response. They can also fail miserably if you use them poorly.

My opinion is that we will see more widespread use of QR codes over the coming two to three years as they are understood by more people and seen on a more regular basis. However, what will give rise to their increased usage will then lead to their death.

Innovative use of QR codes

This is by far my favourite use of a QR code to date, and shows how they can play a pivotal role in multiscreen environments. It's an experiment created by Google and only currently works in their Chrome browser. Essentially, you visit a website on your desktop and when the home page loads it shows a QR code. You scan this code on your mobile device and then the screen on your mobile device can be used to control the contents of the desktop site.

The QR code is just being used as a means to connect your mobile site to a custom-generated URL that then connects the browser on your mobile to the browser on your desktop. This kind of multiscreen interaction offers huge creative opportunities in the world of television and real-world events that have large display screens. Imagine going to a football match, scanning a QR code and being able to interact with what is shown on the stadium screen. A QR code certainly isn't the only mechanism by which this could be achieved, but it is a very practical method currently. Give it a try by visiting the link below on your desktop and then scanning the code with your smartphone: **http://odem.chromeexperiments.com/**.

QR codes: conclusions

The initial growth will be very much fuelled by things like Google Goggles and Google Glass. If you aren't familiar with these products, they both allow you to search visually in some way. Goggles is an app for your phone that allows you to search by taking a picture, and it already offers QR code recognition. As the functionality in this great app gets better and better, more people will use it regularly and more people will have a code scanner to hand regularly. Google Glass is an AR pair of glasses, that overlays useful information and allows you to carry out activities via voice recognition. It's a no-brainer that some form of QR capture would be built into a device like this (although how you go about browsing a website on a device like Google Glass is another question, so we may be looking at capture for later usage).

After this initial growth period though, the same types of products will probably lead to the death of QR codes. We explored AR-based services like Blippar in Chapter 14 but essentially these kinds of tools don't actually require a code, but can recognize things like an entire page of a magazine, which can then do the same things as a QR code. As processing power of mobile devices increases and we see advances in visual search, the need for a code becomes redundant.

There is no reason why my mobile device can't recognize any object, location or anything else, and then show me related online content. Google Goggles is an example of this in practice already. The reality here though is that Google becomes the one deciding what to show you when you scan something and this is where QR codes have their strength. Currently, you create the code and you decide where it drives people. You just need to make sure you have a strong enough value proposition in order to make it work.

16 Near field communication (NFC)

Near field communication (NFC) allows devices to interact via radio frequencies when they are brought into close proximity to one another (normally within a few centimetres). This means that I could touch my mobile device onto an NFC-enabled 'thing' and that touch can launch something, or change something, on my phone. For example, it can be used for making mobile payments using a mobile device (much like 'touchless' credit card technology). It can also be used to launch a mobile website when I touch it onto marketing materials with an NFC chip embedded into it. The object with an NFC-embedded chip that causes my mobile device to react in some way does not require any power, so it can be put into pretty much any object.

The small size of NFC chips means they can be embedded into business cards, as shown in Figure 16.1, whilst Figure 16.2 shows one of the first NFC-enabled print ads. Each ad had an NFC chip stuck to the ad, with a message to scan with your NFC-enabled phone. The reality is that when the ad in Figure 16.2 was published, NFC adoption and usage was very low, but this was as much about innovation as it was about using NFC as a practical marketing tool.

FIGURE 16.1   Business cards with embedded NFC chips (MOO) (www.moo.com)

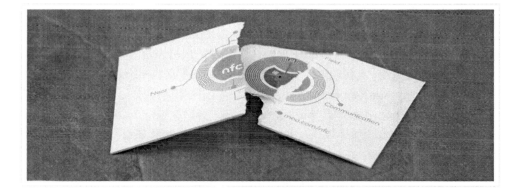

FIGURE 16.2   NFC-enabled print ad in *Wired* magazine

The early NFC elephant in the room

NFC is supposed to be a QR code killer. Why use an ugly QR code for which you need to launch an app before you can even scan it, when you could just touch your phone onto something to do the same thing?

Apart from the limited number of phones that actually support NFC currently, there was initially another major hurdle to their adoption. If you are familiar with Bluetooth on your phone, you are also probably aware that many people switch it off because leaving it on drains your battery. This is also true of NFC on some devices. This was actually addressed fairly quickly on the Android platform and by many handset manufacturers, but it still means some users switch it off. This means if you want to use NFC, you have to go to your phone, switch the NFC on and then touch – not dissimilar to the QR code scan process.

NFC adoption

NFC has been adopted by many of the large handset manufacturers including Sony and Samsung. Sony have even built a number of innovative functionalities into their devices based on the technology, such as one-touch photo-sharing and Xperia tags (discussed more below). However, at the time of writing Apple have not included NFC in their latest iPhones or iPads, and as we have discussed elsewhere in this book, broad adoption of a technology is generally needed to give it enough momentum to get into mainstream usage.

Around half a billion NFC-enabled devices are expected to be in use in 2014 (ABI Research, 2013) and iSuppli predict that 13 per cent of mobile phones shipped will integrate NFC in 2014, up from 4.1 per cent in 2010. These are still relatively low percentages, however, especially considering the cost of implementing something like an NFC print ad.

Mobile payments

It was believed very early on that the 'killer app' for NFC would be mobile payments, with many predicting that our phones would replace credit and debit cards very quickly. The technology already exists to do this, with Google Wallet for example (see Figure 16.3), but adoption has been relatively slow on NFC-enabled phones, with competitive systems (already built into credit cards for example) creating fragmentation and further slowing mobile consumer adoption. However, the potential utility of combining credit cards and smart card payments (like mass transit cards used for underground train

FIGURE 16.3 Google Wallet for NFC payments (www.google.com/wallet)

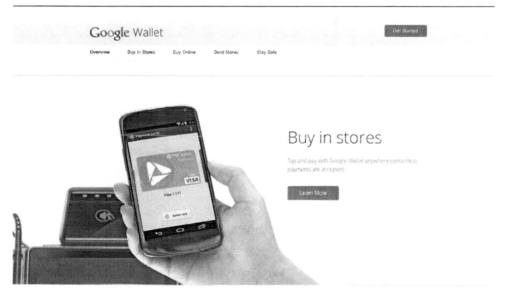

systems) into our mobile devices will help to drive this technology forward.

The other key driver in mobile payments via our phones will be the developing world. Since over 50 per cent of the developing world is 'unbanked' (has no access to banking services) (World Bank, Financial Access Report, 2012), using phones for tracking micro-payments has huge potential and research and development is being funded by the Gates Foundation.

The internet of things

The 'internet of things' is a concept that describes having everyday objects tagged in some way and/or connected to the internet. This means that you could connect to any of these objects at any time and get feedback from any sensors they contained, identify their last physical location or have them interact in some way. An example of this concept in action would be to tag all stock in a supermarket with NFC (or some other technology) so we could track stock as it arrived at the shelf, was scanned at the checkout and then was scanned again as it arrived in the kitchen of the consumer. This could be taken a step further, allowing us to scan again as we placed the packaging into recycling, thus triggering an automatic re-ordering of the product.

Sony's Xperia tags, small coloured discs like key fobs, allow you to trigger customizable behaviour in your phone or tablet when placed near the tag. For example, you can trigger your alarm to be set and your phone to be put onto silent when you place your phone next to the tag on your bedside table. This is a great and early example of objects interacting in some useful way using NFC.

CASE STUDY   Museum of London

Industry

Tourism

Location

UK

Marketing objectives

Provide a richer and more engaging experience for visitors.
Encourage greater loyalty and online sharing by visitors.

Their challenge

The Museum of London wanted to embrace new technologies to enhance the visitor experience at its two venues, the Museum of London and the Museum of London Docklands. The museum already had interactive elements within the two locations but wanted to drive visitors to its Collections Online website, increase its social media followers, raise awareness of exhibitions and its Friends scheme, and drive sales of the museum's guidebook and at its gift shop and restaurant.

Their solution

By utilizing NFC technology, the museum worked with Nokia to create a full suite of interactive tags across the two sites that would allow visitors who had an NFC-enabled phone to engage with various displays.

By merely holding a device up to a share point on the various exhibits, visitors could access more information, hints and tips about other exhibits and vouchers for use in the coffee shop and gift store.

In addition, users could choose to check in on Facebook and Foursquare at various points and follow the museum on Twitter all by a single tap of the screen.

Their results

The museum was one of the first public venues to establish NFC across its sites and the tool enhances the existing interactive elements which have proven their success.

Taking this to the next level and including NFC technology also meant that the interactions were faster than relying on Bluetooth or 3G connections.

What's good about it

The museum managed to find an innovative way of embracing new technology that to date had only been used for making small purchases. It cemented the technology as a tool for engaging with visitors and providing a bridge between the online and offline experience.

The technology can bring together online communities that enhance the visitor experience in real time and add value to the museum customers.

What they said about it

NFC technology has opened up the possibilities of how we can interact with our visitors. By simply touching the tags located throughout our venues, visitors can delve deeper into London's story in an immediate and engaging way, rather than waiting until they get home to find out more about what they've seen.

Vicky Lee, Marketing Manager, Museum of London

Short messaging service (SMS)

17

With news published in April 2013 that the number of messages sent by mobile messaging service apps such as WhatsApp have overtaken the number of messages sent by short messaging service (SMS), many news sites reported the death of SMS. SMS is one of the oldest data transfer methods used on smartphones and many of us feel that too much SMS-based marketing is spammy and interruptive (Text Marketer, 2013).

But let's a take a moment and look at things differently. Over 99 per cent of SMS messages are opened and over 90 per cent of SMS messages are opened within the first three minutes of being received (Tatango, 2013). This is both the blessing and the curse of SMS messages and deserves some further consideration.

SMS is personal

The reason that SMS marketing is disliked, and the reason that 99 per cent of SMS messages are opened, both stem from the fact that SMS is about personal communications and it is interruptive. We use SMS to communicate primarily with our friends, family and colleagues, and it is far more immediate than social media and e-mail marketing because it interrupts us far more directly. An e-mail popping up in the corner of your screen is a lot more subtle than a device in your pocket making a noise and vibrating. For this reason, a poorly targeted SMS message is both inconvenient, because it demands our attention immediately, and is perceived to have intruded into our personal space.

The personal nature of SMS means that as marketers we must be highly selective in how we utilize the technology.

Types of SMS communications

In my personal opinion, you should avoid thinking of SMS marketing in a similar way to e-mail marketing, as a push channel that can allow you to send messages when you want to communicate with a consumer. SMS should be seen as a channel that is only used to send communications exactly when the consumer (again I use the word consumer broadly as including an individual involved in a B2B transaction) wants them.

This means that SMS is most effective if used in one of the following three scenarios:

- **Immediate response** – I request that an SMS is sent to me immediately to provide me with some form of information, whether that is a discount code or a link for an app (discussed further in a moment).

- **Planned timing** – I request an SMS at a particular time. This may be as a reminder of a particular event or contractual obligation.

- **Triggered message** – I request an SMS that is triggered by a certain event or set of circumstances. This could be when a product is shipped, when I reach a certain balance on my credit card, or when somebody tries to log into my social media account incorrectly three times.

There is another scenario, with plenty of evidence that supports its effectiveness, but which I generally will not advise any of my clients to use:

- **Newsletter and promotion messages** – a message that gives news or a special offer to an opt-in telephone number that was not specifically requested. For example, I buy a pizza on my phone via an app, and I am then sent regular messages about deals and discounts.

As I have said, there are plenty of case studies, generally from SMS marketing companies, that show the response rates and revenue generated from these campaigns, and certainly in some very limited circumstances they can be effective. However, SMS is not e-mail, and for every case study showing how well it works, there are a hundred of our friends, family members and colleagues complaining about SMS marketing messages (that is a generalization and one that I am happy to make; I look forward to debating with any SMS marketing companies that disagree!).

SMS is not e-mail. I do not want to be physically interrupted with news and special offers, unless I have specifically asked for them. Although (let's also be clear), nor do I want to be reminded at 4 am, while I am sleeping, that my credit card bill is due. My main advice is to approach SMS marketing with the greatest caution and consideration, and realize how much brand damage you can actually do if you do it carelessly.

SMS short codes

SMS is still the most commonly used data service on all smartphones, and exceeds the percentage of users that will ever use mobile web browsing significantly (Comscore, 2013).

For this reason, using SMS short codes can be a popular mechanism to engage with consumers via other marketing channels. SMS short codes allow marketers to add instructions to print and online marketing, to encourage users to send a message to a particular short code (basically a short telephone number) to receive something in return.

They are commonly used to allow users to enter competitions (and there is often a cost associated with this), to request a discount voucher (often used in the restaurant industry), and to receive a web link with further information on a particular topic.

The main advantage of this approach is that it allows offline marketing a direct link to the consumer. The downside is that it is hard to get users to make the effort to initialize the process and there are often costs associated with sending text messages that can put potential users off.

SMS short codes have been replaced in some cases by things like QR codes and NFC that require less user effort and do not have any associated concerns about cost of usage. Bear in mind though that QR code and NFC adoption rates cannot compete with the more than 75 per cent of smartphone users who regularly use SMS (Comscore, 2013).

> ### SMS campaign examples
>
> As with all of the technologies we discuss in this book, you can find links to the latest stats as well as lots of example campaigns on our website: **http://www.targetinternet.com/mobilemarketing.**

SMS app links

A growing, and very practical, use of SMS is to send links to allow users to download apps to their smartphones. Figure 17.1 illustrates how Bank of America for example uses SMS to help with app download and discovery. This process generally involves having a landing page for an app within a website that is expected to be viewed and discovered on a mobile device. The idea is that a user can identify

FIGURE 17.1   Bank of America: SMS for easy app download (www. bankofamerica.com/online-banking/mobile.go)

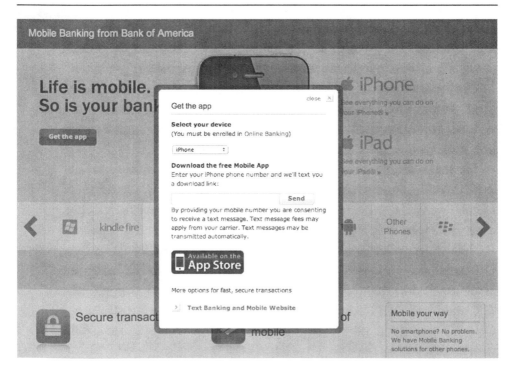

an app on the web, enter their telephone number and be sent a link to download the app directly to their phone, saving them having to try and find the app via one of the main app stores. The other advantage is that it allows the user to preselect the mobile operating system their device uses and provides data to the owner of the website about their interest in the app.

This approach is highly practical, because it fits in nicely with the user journey, saving effort when moving from desktop to a mobile app. Also, and probably most importantly, it aids app discovery. The increasing challenge is to help users find apps in the major app stores that are controlled by the app store owners (most notably Apple and Google) and have huge levels of competition for visibility. This approach means that a search engine-discoverable landing page is created that helps to funnel potential app downloaders directly to the right page in the app store on their mobile device.

SMS: conclusions

Only use SMS when you have a very clear indication that the target audience wants a specific message and always use SMS very cautiously. Consider the advantages of using SMS for app discovery and don't forget that, although short codes aren't new technology, they are one of the few technologies that are used by almost anyone who has a smartphone.

CASE STUDY Feeding Your Kids Foundation

Industry

Not for profit

Location

International

Marketing objectives

Provide parents with knowledge and tools they need to feed their children healthier foods and teach better eating habits.

Their solution

The programme, free to more than 12,000 parents worldwide, powers daily messages featuring region-specific nutritional information and educational resources. In addition to the six-week e-mail programme, parents can also receive time-relevant text messages, providing additional nutrition and wellness information.

The e-mail and SMS campaign was powered by global provider ExactTarget, allowing global location-based targeting of content.

Their results

Some 83 per cent of participants reported learning new ways to improve their children's health.

What's good about it

The campaign was content-focussed, globally run but used region-specific data and mixed e-mail marketing with highly targeted SMS messaging effectively.

What they said about it

Our organization equips parents around the world with the knowledge and tools they need to feed their children healthier foods and teach better eating habits.

Carey White, Chairman, Feeding Your Kids Foundation

By integrating the power of e-mail and SMS, Feeding Your Kids Foundation has successfully connected with its participants, using the channels that work best in each unique interaction, with phenomenal results.

Tim Kopp, Chief Marketing Officer, ExactTarget

Mobile analytics

In this chapter we will explore the huge opportunity that web and mobile analytics give us, and how we can move toward calculating return on investment (ROI) for our mobile marketing.

Mobile analytics means you will no longer ever have the problem of not having enough data to assess your campaigns. Your problem now will be having way too much data and not knowing what to do with it! In most organizations I look at, they now have web and mobile analytics (this is an improvement on where things were a couple of years ago) but the data isn't used in an effective way at all. In fact, the most use that web analytics gets in the majority of organizations is a chart being held up once a month showing web traffic going up. This doesn't say **why** traffic is going up, how it could be improved further, or if in fact it's going up more slowly than the competitors'. The data is just the starting point. To be effective in using mobile marketing we need to be able to analyse that data and use it to measure and improve our efforts.

The marvels of Google Analytics

Google Analytics, the free analytics tool from Google, with over 80 per cent global share of the analytics market (W3Techs, 2013), has hundreds of built-in reports as well as a huge variety of customization options. It is constantly updated and offers a great deal of what many commercial analytics packages offer (and more in some cases!). So one of the most common questions asked is: why is it free?

Google Analytics started out life as a commercial tool called Urchin. This was then purchased by Google, repackaged and given away for free to help website owners improve their sites and drive revenue. Why does Google want you to make more money? Because then you are more likely to spend money on their advertising products, which generate 92 per cent of their income (Google, 2013).

There is in fact a paid version of Google Analytics (Google Analytics Premium) that gives you some of the things absent from the free version, like an account manager, telephone support and service level agreements. It also gives you even more functionality and extended access to data and customization. However, it costs $150,000 per year (this may seem like a huge amount, but actually represents good value when you consider what you get and the fact it is aimed at enterprise-level organizations).

Google Analytics: global use and privacy

For some people and some locations, Google Analytics isn't suitable. For example, it won't work properly in China because of data being blocked leaving the country and users not being able to log in to read their reports. At the time of writing, there are legal challenges from Norway and Germany that state that Google Analytics isn't in compliance with privacy laws. In other cases people just don't like Google or want to share their data with them. If you find yourself in one of these scenarios there are a number of alternatives. There are several excellent commercial options, the market leader of which is Site Catalyst from Adobe. There are also several free alternatives, including the excellent PIWIK. The core principles of analytics remain the same and the majority of the reports we discuss here exist in these other packages as well (sometimes under different names).

Throughout this chapter we will focus on showing how you can use a tool like Google Analytics to help with every stage of your mobile marketing activity. We'll look at using the tools in practice and understand how they can be used within our mobile sites and apps.

Setting up analytics

Most analytics packages use a technique called 'page tagging'. When you register for a Google Analytics account you are given a unique code which needs to be put on every page of your website. This code then sends information back to Google each time somebody uses one of website pages or app screens (see the box below for more on analytics in apps). This data includes a range of mobile-specific reports.

Google Analytics for apps

You can add Google Analytics to apps and get similar reports as you do for a website. Once you have set up an Analytics account you add a new 'property' (a property is a website or an app). Once the app property is set up you are given some unique identifying code which needs to be built into your app. This is more complicated than just adding the code to every page of your website and will need to be done by an app developer.

Once the app is set up, you will get a wide range of reports that we will discuss in more detail later in this chapter. The core thing to understand is that app analytics reports generally talk about screens rather than pages as used in web analytics, but they are very closely aligned. There is also extensive reporting on 'events'. These are things that happen within a screen in your app without the need for another screen to load. You can also look at events in web analytics, but due to the nature of mobile apps, they are more widely used in this scenario.

Core reports

Once you have your analytics code in place, your analytics package will start recording visitors to your website or app. These reports are broken down into a number of different categories. I have highlighted some of the core areas of reports below. After this we will take a look in detail at some of the reports that are most relevant from a mobile marketing perspective.

Real-time

As the name suggests, these reports can show you people using your website or app in real time. You can track where they came from (search engine, other websites etc), what content they are looking at and where they are in the world, amongst other things. One of the key things to remember about real-time reports is that they can be an immensely engaging and utterly useless waste of your time! What I mean is that, although the data is fascinating, and it's thoroughly engaging to see who is using your website in real time, it's not easy to do anything useful with the data. It's great to see the instant reaction to an e-mail going out or a social media campaign, but hard to take away any actionable insights.

Audience

This will tell you all about where in the world your audience is located and, very importantly, about the technology they are using to access your site or app. This will include, through the Devices report, data on the mobile devices on which they are accessing your site, the operating system of those devices, as well as the volume of mobile visitors.

Another useful report for mobile marketing is Visitors Flow report. You can use this to look visually at how people are travelling through your site (Figures 18.1 and 18.2). The great thing about this report is that it is very easy to change the way the audience is initially split up. As standard, you'll see visitors from each country and how they travel through your site, which pages they look at and where they exit. However, it is very easy to change the initial segmentation from country to mobile devices. By doing this you can explore how mobile users travel through your site and see how their behaviour differs from desktop users. This can be useful for identifying pages that may give a poor mobile experience leading to lots of site exits.

FIGURE 18.1 Devices: volume of mobile visitors and devices used (www.google.com/analytics)

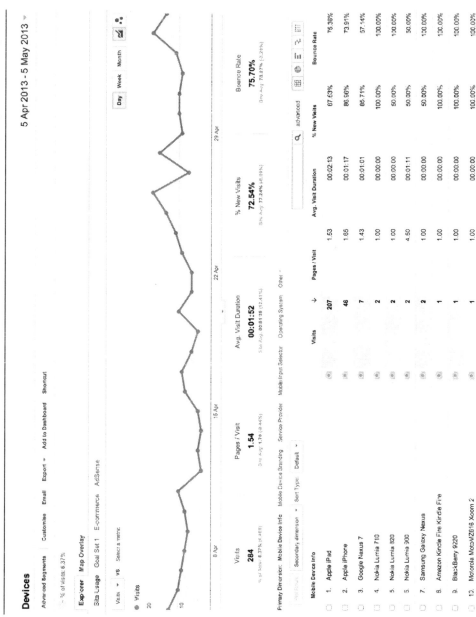

FIGURE 18.2   Visitor Flow report: how mobile users travel through your site

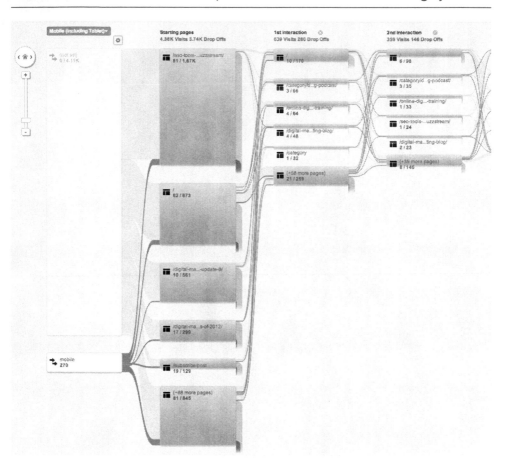

Traffic Sources

These reports will show you where your traffic is coming from and help you identify which of your mobile marketing efforts are helping to drive visitors to your website. You can drill down into each of the different sources of traffic and it will show you traffic from search engines, social media sites, other websites (called Referrals) and direct traffic. Direct traffic is theoretically people that have just typed your website address into their browser or clicked on a bookmark that they have previously saved. The reality is that direct traffic just means that Google cannot identify where the traffic is from. More on this later when we look at tracking code.

Advanced Segments

Advanced Segments is an often missed but hugely powerful feature of Google Analytics that is incredibly useful in mobile marketing. It allows you to select a particular segment of your audience and then see all of the normal reports for that segment. You can also select multiple segments and compare these on the same report. There are pre-defined segments that you can easily select, or with a little knowledge you can build your own custom segments. Happily, 'mobile traffic' is a pre-defined segment, and you can therefore isolate this traffic and use the huge array of reports available to investigate your mobile audience further. You can also compare this against non-mobile visitors very easily. Figure 18.3 shows how Advanced Segments compares your mobile traffic against all other site visitors.

Another feature within the Traffic Sources report allows you to look at your search engine traffic in more detail and understand the different search terms that are driving visitors to your site. By using these reports in combination with Advanced Segments (see Figure 18.4) you can start to understand the different ways in which desktop and mobile users are searching.

You can also look at how different social media sites are sending visitors to your site, and again, by combining this report with use of Advanced Segments, you can see how many of these visitors were on mobile devices (see Figure 18.5).

Under Traffic Sources, you can also examine any traffic you are getting from PPC campaigns that you may be running. If you are using the Google AdWords platform you can connect your Analytics account to your PPC account and you will get full campaign reporting directly in Google Analytics.

It is also worth mentioning here that if you have a Google Webmaster Tools account (something we discussed in Chapter 12), you can also connect this account to your Analytics account and get far more extensive keyword reporting.

FIGURE 18.3 Advanced Segments report: mobile vs other site traffic (www.google.com/analytics)

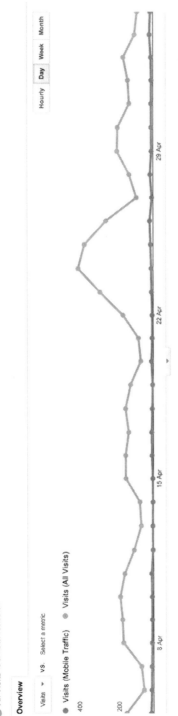
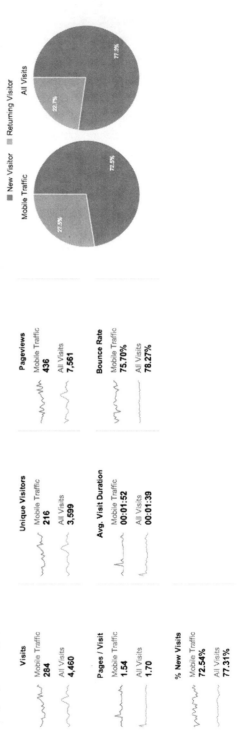

FIGURE 18.4   Traffic Sources + Advanced Segments: search term analysis (www.google.com/analytics)

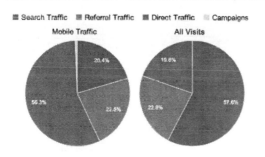

Search Traffic   Referral Traffic   Direct Traffic   Campaigns

Keyword	Visits	% Visits
1. (not provided)		
Mobile Traffic	17	29.31%
All Visits	1,925	74.99%
2. raven tools		
Mobile Traffic	4	6.90%
All Visits	7	0.27%
3. success stories in social media		
Mobile Traffic	3	5.17%
All Visits	3	0.12%
4. daniel rowles digital marketing		
Mobile Traffic	2	3.45%
All Visits	2	0.08%
5. digital advertising podcast		
Mobile Traffic	2	3.45%
All Visits	2	0.08%
6. how to put contact info into qr code		
Mobile Traffic	2	3.45%
All Visits	2	0.08%

Content

As you can probably guess, these reports highlight which of your content is most popular, how long users are staying on particular pages, and look at things like bounce and exit rates. A 'bounce' is somebody entering and exiting a website on the same page; an 'exit' is just the final page in a website visit.

FIGURE 18.5 Traffic Sources + Advanced Segments: social media traffic analysis (www.google.com/analytics)

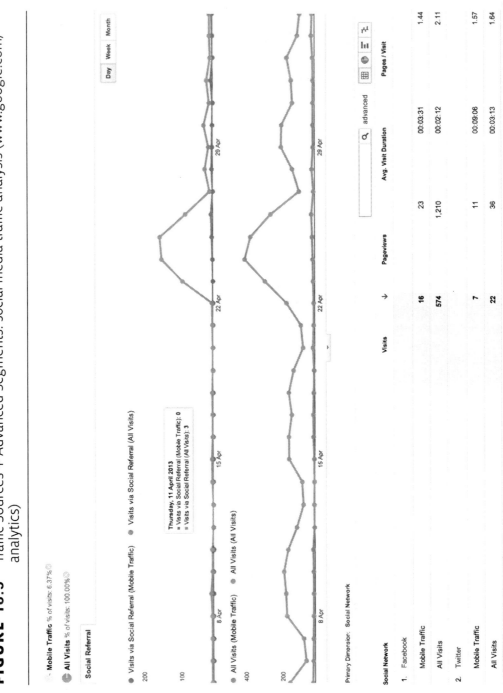

> ### Not all bounces are equal
>
> We generally assume a bounce is a bad thing. For example, someone
> arriving at your website from a search engine, landing on your home page,
> not liking the look of it and then leaving, is a bounce. However, somebody
> bookmarking your blog because they read it every week, landing on your
> blog page, reading it for 25 minutes and then leaving, is also a bounce.
> The visitor still entered and exited your website on the same page. Therefore,
> a bounce isn't always a bad thing if the users have got what they wanted.

Another useful tool under the Content reports is In-page Analytics.
This allows you to actually see your web pages, navigate to an individual page and see the particular data for that page. It doesn't currently give you the option to view your site as if on a mobile device,
but I was assured by Google in April 2013 that this feature is already
in production.

Conversions

This is the single most important set of reports within Analytics,
because it is the most closely aligned with your business objectives.
A conversion is somebody completing one of your online goals. As
standard analytics will not have any goals set up, in order to get the
most out of your Analytics package you really need to set up some goals.

A goal is a user doing something you want them to do. That could
be making a purchase, filling in a lead generation form, clicking on
an ad, listening to a podcast or any number of other things that may
be aligned with your end business objectives. You can set up these
goals within the admin functionality of Analytics and it's worth
understanding the different types of goals you can set up:

- **URL destination** – a visitor getting to a particular page. Quite
  often a 'thank you' page, such as thank you for buying, thank
  you for downloading etc. We know if someone gets to one of
  these pages they have carried out an action and we can track
  this as a goal.

- **Visit duration** – you may decide that somebody staying on your site for a certain period of time indicates they are using your content and this can help when your goal may be awareness.

- **Pages per visit** – you may decide that somebody looking at a certain number of pages during a visit to your site is a goal for you. Always remember though that this could mean somebody cannot find what they are looking for and are trawling through the content of your site looking for it.

- **Event** – an event is something that happens within a page, like somebody clicking on a link to an external website, or filling in a field on a form. We can also track these things within a page. However, this requires additional code to be added to your web pages for each event you are tracking.

Once these goals are set up we will start to get Goal Reports. These show all of the goals completed and can again be used in conjunction with Advanced Segments to isolate goals completed on mobile devices. Figure 18.6 shows a Goal Report with Advanced Segments to separate goals completed on mobile devices and desktops.

Multi-Channel Funnels

One of the limitations of Goal Reports is that they take a 'last-click' approach. This means that if you look at the source of a report, it will tell you which traffic sources deliver the visitor to your site. For example, if you did a search in Google, came to my site and then filled in a form, the source of the goal would be a search. The problem becomes clear though if we take another example. How about you receive an e-mail, visit my website, then a week later you do a search and then you fill in a form. Again, the source of the conversion would be given as the search, but clearly the e-mail has also contributed.

This is where the very powerful Multi-Channel Funnels comes in. These reports tell you all of the different sources of traffic that contributed towards your goals being completed. So, for example, if lots of users are visiting via social media sites, but then visiting again

FIGURE 18.6 Goal Report + Advanced Segments: completed mobile vs desktop goals (www.google.com/analytics)

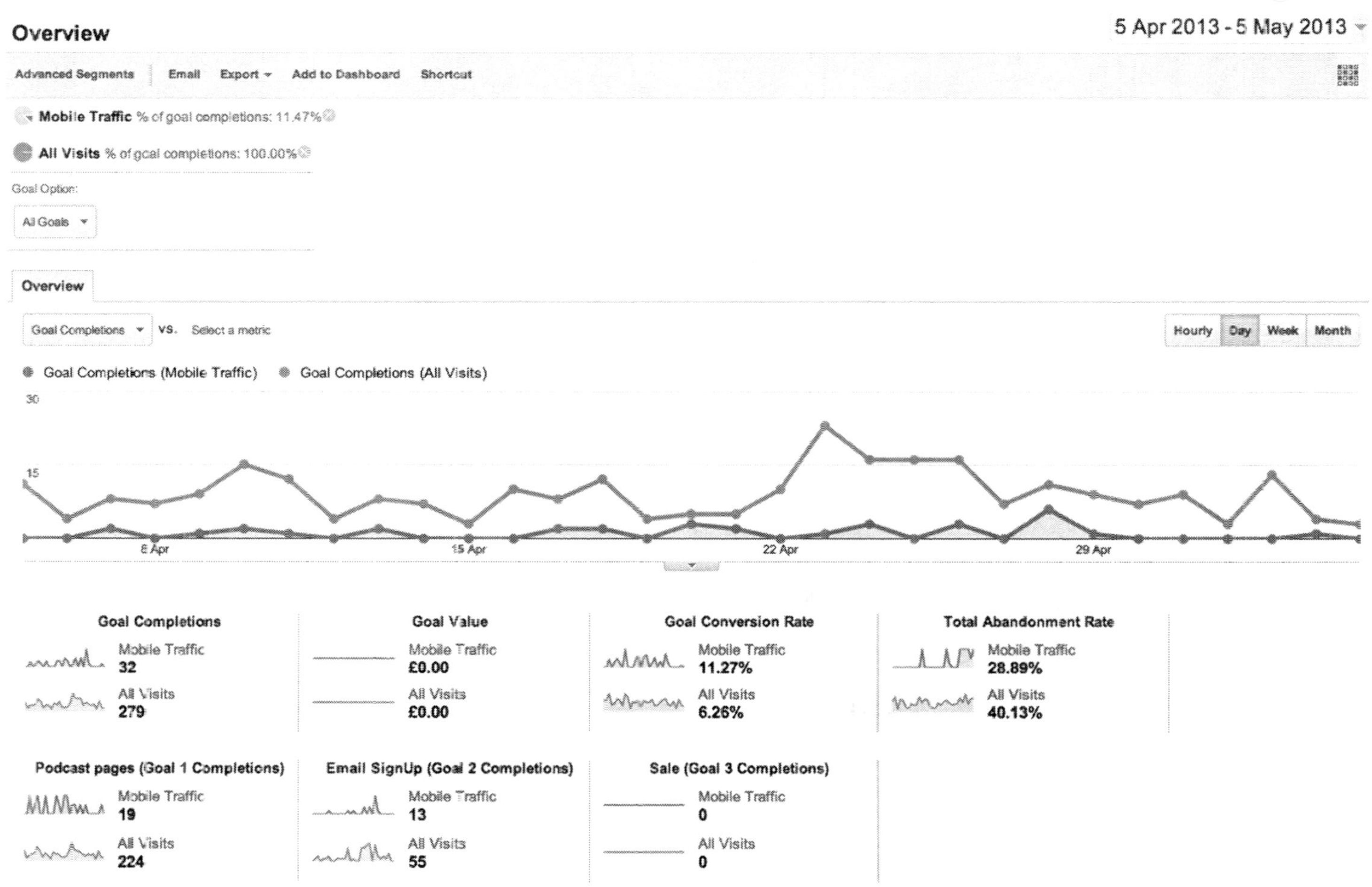

Overview

Advanced Segments | Email | Export ▾ | Add to Dashboard | Shortcut

5 Apr 2013 - 5 May 2013 ▾

● Mobile Traffic % of goal completions: 11.47%

● All Visits % of goal completions: 100.00%

Goal Option:

All Goals ▾

Hourly | Day | Week | Month

Overview

Goal Completions ▾ vs. Select a metric

● Goal Completions (Mobile Traffic) ● Goal Completions (All Visits)

30

15

6 Apr   15 Apr   22 Apr   29 Apr

Goal Completions
Mobile Traffic
32
All Visits
279

Goal Value
Mobile Traffic
£0.00
All Visits
£0.00

Goal Conversion Rate
Mobile Traffic
11.27%
All Visits
6.26%

Total Abandonment Rate
Mobile Traffic
28.89%
All Visits
40.13%

Podcast pages (Goal 1 Completions)
Mobile Traffic
19
All Visits
224

Email SignUp (Goal 2 Completions)
Mobile Traffic
13
All Visits
55

Sale (Goal 3 Completions)
Mobile Traffic
0
All Visits
0

via search and then completing my goals, these reports will identify this for me (see Figure 18.7). They will tell me what percentage of all of my conversions has involved each of the different traffic sources, even if it wasn't the final click before conversion. This can be hugely powerful in starting to understand the overall user journey in more detail, and how each of your different marketing activities is actually contributing towards your goals being achieved.

FIGURE 18.7   Multi-Channel Funnels: understanding the user journey (www.google.com/analytics)

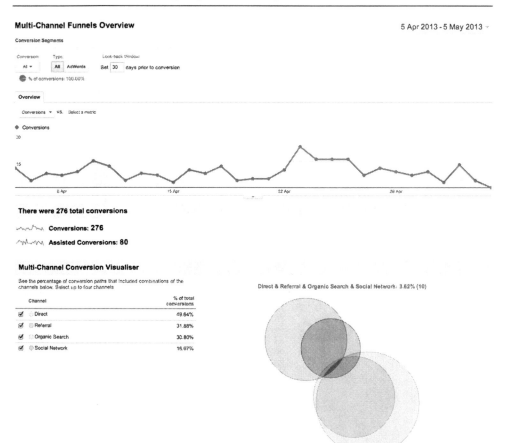

Hands-on learning resources for Analytics

Reading about Analytics is one thing, but when you come to try each of these reports out you may need a little more help. I've listed my favourite two analytics learning resources below. Both are from Google and both are free:

- Google Analytics IQ Lessons – these interactive online tutorials walk you through the core reports of analytics in a very clear way: **http://www.google.co.uk/analytics/iq.html**

- Google Analytics YouTube Channel – this is an absolute goldmine of analytics tutorials and explanations. It also includes the excellent Web Analytics TV, featuring the hugely talented Avinash Kaushik and Nick Mihailovski answering lots of user questions about Google Analytics: **http://www.youtube.com/user/googleanalytics**.

App-specific reports

Many of the reports that apply to websites also apply to app analytics but will be read slightly differently. For example, you can track all of the items below once analytics is running within your app:

- number of app installations;
- devices and networks used to access app;
- geographic location and languages spoken by visitors;
- in-app purchase totals;
- customized tracking of app content, like video;
- number of screens seen per visit.

Tracking code

In order to track some sources of traffic through to your site you may need to use some analytics tracking code. This can be particularly useful if you are placing different versions of an ad on different devices for example. Tracking code is added to a web link, and then when the traffic source is shown, the details you have entered will be given. Let's walk through an example to make sense of this.

If I place a link in my e-mail that drives traffic to my website without adding tracking code, the traffic from the e-mail will show up as direct traffic. The reason for this is that when a user clicks on a link in an e-mail, Google doesn't generally know where that click has come from (unless we are talking about web mail). Therefore, to really understand our e-mail visitors we need to add tracking code to all of our links so we can separate where the traffic has come from and analyse it properly.

Generating traffic code is very straightforward and thankfully Google gives us a tool to simplify things. First of all just search 'Google URL builder'. You'll find the Google URL builder (which is just an online form for generating tracking code). You enter the page you want to link to, fill in a couple of fields and it will generate a new link for you that includes your original link and appends the tracking code. Now, if you add this to your e-mail, when somebody clicks on the link it will be reported in Google Analytics as 'Campaign Traffic' along with the name you gave it and any other details entered into the URL builder.

This can be used to generate tracking code for e-mails, online ads, links in social media sites and so on, and can help you track a particular link and the traffic it is driving to your site.

Mobile data and the Modern Marketing Manifesto

I spoke to Ashley Friedlein, CEO of Econsultancy, about why he thinks data is such an essential part of mobile marketing and why it was given key positioning in The Modern Marketing Manifesto. Ashley told me:

> The problem with the term 'mobile marketing' is that it sounds like the focus is on the device and the technology, rather than using mobile technology as an enabler. It also makes it sound like a stand-alone discipline. We have always maintained that mobile marketing, and digital marketing generally, does not exist in isolation. It is part of the bigger whole that is marketing. But digital has undeniably brought new aspects to that whole. So what if we were to reconstitute marketing as it is today with digital and classic fully fused? What would that look like?

He went on to explain something that Econsultancy has recently completed and taken to market that specifically tries to promote the use of data in marketing (amongst other key topics):

> In order to answer these questions we created the Modern Marketing Manifesto. Its aim is to outline why we believe marketing is increasingly valuable and to define what it is to be a modern marketer. We see that the effective use of data is essential to business success.

Below is the excerpt on data from the Manifesto:

> **Data**
>
> We believe data must be turned into insight and action to be a source of customer, competitive and marketing advantage. Data is the bedrock upon which successful research, segmentation, marketing automation, targeting and personalisation are built.
>
> Data allows us to predict future behaviour which is fundamental to creating strong customer lifetime value models and optimising marketing effectiveness. Digital channels provide new and valuable sources of data and customer insight that can be acted upon in real time.
>
> If you do not see data as exciting, valuable and empowering then you are not a modern marketer.

That last sentence is my favourite. It makes me feel less of a geek for getting so excited about analytics and the insights we can glean from it!

I think another thing worth highlighting in the Manifesto (the whole thing is excellent and very worthy of your time), especially when we are focussing on mobile marketing, is that technology is an enabler, not the point. I have argued several times in this book that the term mobile marketing can make us focus too much on a device, and I think the further excerpt from the Manifesto below sums up that point nicely.

> **Technology**
>
> We believe technology is an enabler rather than a solution in itself. But modern marketers must be comfortable and adept at procuring and using technology to their best advantage.
>
> We believe modern marketers will have increasing ownership of technology at the same time as technologists become more marketing-aligned.

You can read the whole Manifesto on the excellent Econsultancy blog. It's one of my most trusted sources of up-to-date digital marketing news and they publish regular news on mobile marketing: **http://econsultancy.com/uk/blog/62668-our-modern-marketing-manifesto-will-you-sign**.

PART THREE
Mobile marketing checklists

Introduction

Part Three of this book is aimed at helping you implement the different elements of your mobile marketing strategy. The checklists will give you a step-by-step approach to planning and implementing the different elements of your strategy and highlight the key things you need to think about.

We started this book by talking about the importance of understanding the environment you are working in and setting clear objectives for your mobile activity. The aim of Part Three is to streamline this process and give you an easy framework to work within. The checklists highlight the key steps involved, without being too prescriptive and limiting your creative ideas. They should help you avoid missing any key issues and remember the steps that will save you lots of time and potential stress.

We start with an overall mobile strategy checklist and then provide checklists for each of the core mobile technologies and channels. The strategy checklist should be your first step. Once you feel you have ticked each of the appropriate steps off your list, you can then select the appropriate tactical checklists depending on the technologies you are using to implement your strategy.

A universal framework

Each of the checklists follows a universal framework which you can also apply to any other part of your mobile marketing, or in fact any marketing, activity. This is not supposed to be a detailed strategy model, but rather a simple and easy-to-remember checklist approach that makes sure you have considered the key steps.

Benchmark

Understand the environment you are working within. This will include things like understanding your market, the target audience, the potential user journey, the broad technology options available, how your current activity fits in and any competition.

Objectives

Be clear about what you are actually trying to achieve. This step should give you clarity about the overall objectives of any mobile activity and should be aligned with a clear perspective on how these objectives can be measured. Not only will this help you judge the success of your campaigns, it will also make improving them much easier.

Tactics and technology

Select the most appropriate tactics and technology to achieve your objectives. The benchmarking and objective-setting phases of the process should help inform this stage and give you a clear view of what the most appropriate (or at least potentially useful) tactical approach will be. You also need to consider resourcing and implementation issues at this stage.

Analysis

Access, iterate and improve. Rather than being seen as a final stage, this should be regarded as a way of measuring our tactical implementation against our objectives and looking at ways to improve things. This relies on creating a clear measurement framework when we first set objectives.

For those who like acronyms, I think that BOTA (for benchmark, objectives, tactics and analysis) is simple enough to be remembered easily, and can give us some simple clarity on what is essential to our mobile marketing success. We have applied it throughout this section
and hopefully you can see how it can be adopted as needed for different stages of your mobile marketing planning.

Checklists

20

Mobile marketing strategy

Benchmark

- understand the user journey and how mobile is part of this;
- assess the current level of traffic to your sites via mobile and devices used;
- assess the current site/app experience on mobile devices and identify issues and problems;
- look at the social media user experience on mobile devices;
- analyse competitor sites and apps;
- analyse search experience on mobile devices;
- assess mobile e-mail experience.

Objectives

- set clear objectives of what your primary objectives are (online sales, drive offline sales etc);
- understand any secondary objectives such as building audience and engagement and understand how these contribute to your primary objectives;
- set measures against primary and secondary objectives.

Technology and mix

- consider how other online and offline channels will interact with mobile and map out all possible scenarios for mobile use;
- select the appropriate mobile technologies to fulfil this journey.

Analytics and measurement

- set up analytics and measurement tools for all channels;

- define how measures contribute towards primary and secondary objectives;

- identify opportunities for optimization and improvement;

- measure, analyse, improve, iterate.

Mobile site development

Benchmark

- understand the user journey and how your mobile site is part of this;

- understand user requirements and needs, and assess how the site can deliver on these;

- assess the current level of traffic to your sites via mobile and which devices are used;

- assess the current site experience on mobile devices and identify issues and problems;

- look at current site analytics and understand current user journey, popular content, drop out points etc;

- assess your competitor's mobile site experience.

Objectives

- define how mobile site contributes toward primary business objectives;

- set clear measurable objectives for site and tie in with measurement approach.

User journey

- understand how site is part of user journey and define content and interaction requirements;

- look at use cases, content requirements, personas and other tools to help further define user requirements and align with site content, navigation, interaction and visual design;

- optimize user experience on mobile to deliver maximum opportunity to meet user requirements.

Devices and testing

- build site in appropriate way to give optimized experience on mobile devices;

- consider the impact of building responsive websites on your content management system and other existing infrastructure;

- test on appropriate devices.

Measurement

- set up analytics on mobile sites;

- identify conversion points on site that can be defined as analytics goals;

- define tiered levels of measures (by importance) that contribute to, or are indicators of, primary objectives.

Building your app

Benchmark

- understand the user journey and how your app is part of this;

- understand which devices your target audience is using;

- understand user requirements and needs, and assess how the app can deliver on this;.

- assess any competitors' mobile app experience.

Objectives

- define how your app contributes towards primary business objectives;

- set clear measurable objectives for app and tie in with measurement approach.

User journey

- understand how app is part of user journey and define content and interaction requirements;

- look at use cases, content requirements, personas and other tools to help further define user requirements and align with app content, navigation, interaction and visual design;

- optimize user experience on app to deliver maximum opportunity to meet user requirements.

Devices and testing

- define requirements for either web app or native app;

- define operating system requirements;

- test on appropriate devices.

App marketing

- complete app submission process;

- define complete app marketing plan to increase visibility and drive downloads and positive review;

- engage with audience and moderate feedback;

- improve app and resource ongoing maintenance.

Measurement

- set up analytics within apps;

- identify conversion points on site that can be defined as analytics goals;

- define tiered levels of measures (by importance) that contribute to, or are indicators of, primary objectives;

- analyse analytics, test and improve.

Social media and mobile

Benchmark

- understand how social media is part of the user journey and which platforms are being used by your target audience;
- look at existing social media experience on mobile devices and identify problems and issues;
- benchmark current social media audiences for volume, engagement level, traffic driven to sites and app downloads generated;
- assess competitors' social media platforms and content;
- identify content requirements.

Objectives

- define how social media contributes towards primary business objectives;
- set clear measurable objectives for social media and tie in with measurement approach.

Channels and user experience

- select appropriate social channels based on user journey;
- make sure all social media posting is assessed for mobile users.

Measurement

- go beyond volume and look at engagement, site traffic generation and site goal completion;
- look at overall contribution of social to site goals using 'multi-channel funnels' or similar analytics tool.

Mobile search

Benchmark

- assess your current level of search optimization readiness;
- make sure search engine spiders can access your pages.

Keyword research

- use keyword research tools to identify key phrases that you need to rank for;
- identify differences between desktop and mobile search phrases.

On-page optimization

- get your identified phrases on the pages in the appropriate places:
  - page name (URL)
  - page titles
  - headings and sub-headings
  - copy
  - links
  - alt text
- make sure mobile site pages have appropriate on-page optimization as well as desktop versions.

Links and social signals

- define link-building strategy focussed on providing useful and engaging content;
- drive social media engagement to create social signals to boost search rankings.

Analytics and measurement

- benchmark your current rankings for identified search terms;
- benchmark your current inbound links;
- assess user journey from search terms through your sites and tie in with assessment of site goals;
- look at overall contribution of search to site goals using 'multi-channel funnels' or similar analytics tool;
- adjust keywords and on-page optimization according to results.

Conclusions

I started this book by saying that the truth of mobile marketing lay somewhere between it being 'the year of mobile' and 'mobile marketing is dead'. Well now I'm going to argue that the latter point is correct and explain why that is a good thing!

You may be thinking, 'Why are you telling me mobile is dead? I've just spent hours reading your book on the topic!' It's because mobile is not a stand-alone topic. It is search, social media, content and everything else. What it comes down to is the user journey and understanding context.

We discussed in Chapter 12 on mobile search that Google has changed its paid search system to allow you to focus on the context of a search, rather than purely focussing on the device itself. This approach frames why we need to think about mobile marketing more broadly. It's not about the device; it's about the user journey and the context of that journey.

As the variety of mobile devices increases and the environment we work in becomes more complex, we need to focus on something other than the technology when planning our mobile marketing. Understanding the user journey is key to this, as it allows us to focus on context rather than technology.

Many organizations claim to be focussed on the needs of their target audience. Most aren't. The increasing impact of mobile means that organizations that don't truly understand their audiences and the multi-device journey they are taking online will fail.

Focus on core business objectives and marketing principles, apply the appropriate technology by understanding the user journey, and then measure and improve against your defined objectives. That's it.

I wish you the very best of luck with your mobile marketing efforts and really encourage you to get in contact.

Twitter: @danielrowles
E-mail: danielrowles@me.com

Latest reports, trends and case studies

Don't forget that we have compiled a huge range of resources on mobile marketing on our site and this is updated regularly. You can also download our digital marketing podcasts. The site is of course responsively designed for your mobile devices and we have a web app you can add to your device: **http://www.targetinternet.com/mobilemarketing**.

REFERENCES

Chapter 2: Understanding the mobile consumer

Mobile usage
http://hbr.org/2013/01/how-people-really-use-mobile/

Hotels.com Freefall video
http://www.youtube.com/watch?v=Q7eHinI95rc

Travel and mobile devices
http://thinkdigital.travel/knowledgestream/mobile-drives-traffic-to-travel-sites/

Local search intent
http://www.themobileplaybook.com/

Procter & Gamble FMOT
http://www.pg.com/en_US/downloads/investors/annual_reports/2006/
    pg2006annualreport.pdf

Percentage of users using online reviews
http://www.wtmlondon.com/files/6328_wtm_global_trends_2012_v7_lo1.pdf

Chapter 3: Technology change and adoption

Figure 3.1 http://en.wikipedia.org/wiki/File:DynaTAC8000X.jpg

Comscore Mobile Future in Focus Report
http://www.comscore.com/Insights/Presentations_and_Whitepapers/
    2012/2012_Mobile_Future_in_Focus

China 3G penetration http://www.forbes.com/sites/chuckjones/2013/02/24/
    china-carriers-smartphone-3g-penetration-only-at-22/

Informa 3G UK penetration
http://mobithinking.com/mobile-marketing-tools/latest-mobile-stats/b

German smartphone adoption
http://www.emarketer.com/Article/Western-Europe-Internet-Behavior-
    Differences-Slight-Significant/1009019

Growth in China Baidu search
http://www.techinasia.com/baidu-1100-percent-growth-in-mobile-searches-
    2010-to-2012/

Mobile usage differences
http://mobithinking.com/mobile-marketing-tools/latest-mobile-stats/

Nielsen: Mobile Consumer Report
http://www.nielsen.com/content/dam/corporate/us/en/reports-downloads/
    2013%20Reports/Mobile-Consumer-Report-2013.pdf

Chapter 4: Disruption and integration

Better deals via mobile
http://www.mobilecommercedaily.com/87pc-of-retailers-agree-shoppers-
    can-find-better-deals-via-mobile-survey

Willingness to pay for content
http://www.nielsen.com/us/en/newswire.html?p=31156

Chapter 5: Devices, platforms and technology

Loading times
http://blog.kissmetrics.com/loading-time/

Chapter 6: Mobile statistics

Mobile usage

http://gs.statcounter.com
http://www.itu.int/en/ITU-D/Statistics/Documents/facts/
    ICTFactsFigures2013.pdf

http://ansonalex.com/infographics/smartphone-usage-statistics-and-trends-
    2013-infographic/

http://www.comscore.com/Insights/Press_Releases/2013/3/comScore_
    Reports_January_2013_U.S._Smartphone_Subscriber_Market_Share

http://www.russiansearchtips.com/category/mobile-marketing-in-russia/

http://www.portioresearch.com/en/blog/2013/01/windows-gaining-os-market-share-in-europe-in-2012-and-beyond.aspx

http://stats.areppim.com/stats/stats_mobiosxtime_sam.htm

QR Code Adoption

http://s3.amazonaws.com/pb-web/pdf/smb/pitney-bowes-2012-qr-codes-use-us-europe-report.pdf

http://www.emarketer.com/Article/US-Ahead-of-Western-Europe-QR-Code-Usage/1009631

Mobile OS usage

http://www.itu.int/en/ITU-D/Statistics/Documents/facts/ICTFactsFigures2013.pdf

http://ansonalex.com/infographics/smartphone-usage-statistics-and-trends-2013-infographic/

http://www.comscore.com/Insights/Press_Releases/2013/3/comScore_Reports_January_2013_U.S._Smartphone_Subscriber_Market_Share

http://www.russiansearchtips.com/category/mobile-marketing-in-russia/

http://www.portioresearch.com/en/blog/2013/01/windows-gaining-os-market-share-in-europe-in-2012-and-beyond.aspx

http://stats.areppim.com/stats/stats_mobiosxtime_sam.htm

https://s3.amazonaws.com/pb-web/pdf/smb/pitney-bowes-2012-qr-codes-use-us-europe-report.pdf

Mobile social media

http://www.youtube.com/yt/press/statistics.html

http://www.linkedin.com/groups/In-Japan-consumer-adoption-rate-4094547.S.197462404

http://gs.statcounter.com/#social_media-US-monthly-201203-201303-bar

Trends usage

http://www.newmediatrendwatch.com/

http://www.budde.com.au/Research/Latest-Annual-Publications.aspx

http://trends.e-strategyblog.com/2013/03/01/global-mcommerce-
activities/8919

Chapter 7: The future of mobile

Game to control objects using brain waves
http://gizmodo.com/5396971/the-mindflex-brainwave-game-gives-me-
a-headache

Chapter 9: Mobile sites and responsive design

Website visits on mobile devices
http://www.walkersands.com/quarterlymobiletraffic

Mobile-optimized sites average order values (AOVs)
http://econsultancy.com/uk/blog/62222-how-mobile-optimized-sites-
drive-conversion-rates-and-aovs

Chapter 10: How to build an app

Apple downloads
http://www.forbes.com/sites/markrogowsky/2013/05/03/apple-as-the-app-
store-nears-50-billion-downloads-the-birds-remain-angry-and-popular/

Users prefer apps
http://offers2.compuware.com/APM_13_WP_Mobile_App_Survey_
Report_Registration.html

Nike Training Club
http://www.nike.com/us/en_us/c/womens-training/apps/nike-training-club

Chapter 11: Social media and mobile

Social media usage
http://www.telegraph.co.uk/technology/mobile-phones/9365085/
Smartphones-hardly-used-for-calls.html

http://www.slideshare.net/FlurryMobile/mobile-outlook-2013

Concerns over privacy
http://www.statista.com/statistics/191946/percentage-of-us-
americans-concerned-with-privacy-on-facebook/

Tweets per day
http://blogs.adobe.com/socialpractice/optimize-your-tweets/

Twitter mobile usage
http://marketingland.com/twitter-60-percent-of-users-access-via-mobile-13626

Google Analytics usage
http://techcrunch.com/2012/04/12/google-analytics-officially-at-10m/

Facebook profits on mobile
http://news.sky.com/story/1085750/facebook-results-mobile-ads-boost-revenue

Facebook ads opt-out
http://www.theatlanticwire.com/technology/2013/05/facebook-mobile-
ads/64802/

Facebook under pressure
http://www.telegraph.co.uk/technology/facebook/10030649/
Facebook-under-pressure-to-deliver-on-mobile-growth.html

Chapter 12: Mobile search

Mobile search growth
http://searchengineland.com/mobile-seo-is-not-a-myth-8-popular-
claims-refuted-141386

Growth in China Baidu search
http://www.techinasia.com/baidu-1100-percent-growth-in-mobile-
searches-2010-to-2012/

Google mobile spiders
http://support.google.com/webmasters/bin/answer.py?hl=en&answer=
1061943

Mobile search intent
http://www.seomoz.org/ugc/5-mobile-seo-tips-from-the-google-adwords-team

Search leads to action
http://www.researchscape.com/technology/130319_mobile_searches

Local search-based phone calls
http://searchengineland.com/google-click-to-call-keeping-it-simple-40324

Chapter 13: Mobile advertising

Rising Stars ad formats
http://www.iab.net/risingstarsmobile

IAB
http://www.iab.net

MMA
http://www.mmaglobal.com

Chapter 14: Augmented reality (AR) and real-world integration

Blippar
http://www.blippar.com/

Google Glass
http://www.google.com/glass/start/

Foursquare
https://foursquare.com/

Chapter 15: Quick response (QR) codes

QR code global adoption

http://www.qrstuff.com/blog/?s=qr+code+trends

http://www.emarketer.com/newsroom/index.php/report-shows-
    adoption-qr-codes/

http://www.comscore.com/Insights/Press_Releases/2012/9/QR_Code_
Usage_Among_European_Smartphone_Owners_Doubles_Over_
Past_Year

http://ssl.aip-global.com/EN/asia_express/archives/795

PPC comparison

http://searchenginewatch.com/article/2200730/Organic-vs.-Paid-
Search-Results-Organic-Wins-94-of-Time

http://www.wordstream.com/blog/ws/2012/07/17/google-advertising

Chapter 16: Near field communication (NFC)

NFC adoption
http://www.abiresearch.com/press/nfc-installed-base-to-exceed-500m-
devices-within-1

NFC predicted growth
http://www.digikey.com/us/en/techzone/wireless/resources/articles/
Cell-Phones-with-NFC-Set.html

Google wallet adoption
http://www.bloomberg.com/news/2012-03-21/google-said-to-rethink-
wallet-strategy-amid-slow-adoption.html

Chapter 17: Short messaging service (SMS)

Messenger apps overtake SMS
http://www.bbc.co.uk/news/business-22334338

SMS consumer attitudes
http://www.textmarketer.co.uk/blog/2012/08/sms-marketing-ideas/
consumer-attitudes-to-sms-marketing-infographic/

SMS open rates
http://www.tatango.com/blog/sms-open-rates-exceed-99/

SMS vs other data services usage
http://www.tatango.com/blog/sms-usage-remains-high-in-2012/

SMS adoption rates
http://www.comscore.com/Insights/Press_Releases/2013/1/comScore_
    Reports_November_2012_U.S._Mobile_Subscriber_Market_Share

Chapter 18: Mobile analytics

Google Analytics market share
http://w3techs.com/technologies/details/ta-googleanalytics/all/all

The Modern Marketing Manifesto
http://econsultancy.com/uk/blog/62668-our-modern-marketing-manifesto-
    will-you-sign

Google Revenue
http://investor.google.com/earnings/2013/Q1_google_earnings.html

INDEX

(*italics* indicate a figure or table in the text)

CPSIA information can be obtained at www.ICGtesting.com
Printed in the USA
BVOW04s1229091013

333315BV00004B/4/P